MODERN THEOLOGY

5. Dietrich Bonhoeffer

MODERN THEOLOGY

Selections from twentieth-century theologians
edited with an introduction and notes by

E. J. TINSLEY

5

Dietrich Bonhoeffer

1906–45

LONDON

EPWORTH PRESS

ACKNOWLEDGEMENTS

The author and publisher are grateful for permission to quote in this series from the following works:

Church Dogmatics, Vol. I, 2; IV, 2, T. and T. Clark
Deliverance to the Captives, by Karl Barth, SCM Press
Kerygma and Myth, Vol. I; II, edited by H. W. Bartsch, SPCK
Christology, by Dietrich Bonhoeffer, Collins Publishers
Ethics, by Dietrich Bonhoeffer, SCM Press
Letters and Papers from Prison, by Dietrich Bonhoeffer, SCM Press
Sanctorum Communio, by Dietrich Bonhoeffer, Collins Publishers
The Cost of Discipleship, by Dietrich Bonhoeffer, SCM Press
Form Criticism, by Bultmann and Kundsin, Harper and Row, New York
Theology of the New Testament, Vol. II, by Rudolf Bultmann, translated by F. Grobel, SCM Press
Word and Faith, by G. Ebeling, translated by J. W. Leitch, SCM Press
The Nature of Faith, by Gerhard Ebeling, Collins Publishers
Selections from Karl Barth's Church Dogmatics, by H. Gollwitzer, T. and T. Clark
The Systematic Theology of Paul Tillich, by A. J. McKelway, Lutterworth Press
Beyond Tragedy, by Reinhold Niebuhr, James Nisbet and Co. Ltd
Leaves from the Notebook of a Tamed Cynic, by Reinhold Niebuhr, Harper and Row, New York
The Nature and Destiny of Man, Vol. I; II, by Reinhold Niebuhr, James Nisbet and Co. Ltd
World Come of Age, edited by R. Gregor Smith, Collins Publishers
The Death of God, by Gabriel Vahanian, George Braziller, Inc., New York

CONTENTS

PREFACE TO THE SERIES

The theologians represented in this series of five volumes of selections are those who, one can confidently say, are already assured of an important place in the history of twentieth-century theology.

In the case of each theologian I have tried to give a fair representation of the author's work although, inevitably, there are important aspects of his thought which I have not always found it possible to illustrate. I have throughout preferred to give substantial selections rather than short extracts because the qualities of the writing of the theologians in this collection require this treatment for proper understanding and illustration. Even so selections are no substitute for the original, and it is my hope that readers will become sufficiently interested in what is given in this series to want to go to the full range of the authors' complete works.

As well as being representative of an influential group of theologians I hope that the selections provided will be found to provide something of an integrated discussion among the writers themselves. I have, therefore, in making the selections included some which give an idea how these theologians view each other. The reader is given some indication of the views, say, of Barth on Bultmann or Niebuhr on Barth, and there are cross-references in the introduction and notes so that he can have an idea of what subjects have been of continuing importance in modern theological discussion.

I have made this selection not only for those who have a professional interest in the study of theology (clergy and ministers, teachers, students) but also for the interested member of the general public who, whether believer or not, wishes to have a guide to a reading of some important phases of twentieth-century theology. A general introduction attempts to set the scene and for each author there is a biographical note and brief introductions to the selected passages. In each case also there are suggestions for further study and reading.

University of Leeds   JOHN TINSLEY

INTRODUCTION TO THE SERIES

In this introductory chapter an attempt will be made to explain how the present theological situation in western Europe and the United States has come about. We shall trace very briefly the pedigree of contemporary ideas and attitudes. 'Theology' however is a word (like, e.g., 'mysticism', 'romanticism', 'philosophy') which is frequently and easily used without its meaning having first been made clear. It is not uncommon to find politicians and other public speakers using the word 'theology' to mean some recondite, antiquarian and hopelessly irrelevant intellectual pursuit involving, it is implied, a sad waste of mental energy. It is essential therefore to try first to clarify the meaning of the term 'theology'. A good way of doing this is to describe how theology is done. By describing the process of theology we shall more easily come to an understanding of what it essentially is.

Perhaps there have been as many attempts at a definition of theology as, for example, of art. The comparison with art is very relevant because theology is in one aspect, and a very important one, an instance of the perennial task of working with words to achieve lucidity and precision described by T. S. Eliot as 'the intolerable wrestle with words and meanings'. Even if we think we have found a more or less satisfactory language very often the cultural situation will have meantime so moved on that we find, in Eliot's words again, that we have only learned to get better words for the things we no longer want to say.

Nevertheless theologians have to keep on with this task not because they believe that it is possible, for instance, to describe 'God' or to find a language about God which is valid for all time, but because they believe that theology is a perennial human task. Man is a 'theologizing' animal: i.e., he must be constantly attempting to achieve in a significant pattern of words (or of words together with gestures and sound, as, for example, in liturgy) some way of rationalizing all those facets of his experience and history which point to a meaning beyond the visible and material. Because the most significant activity in religion, worship, involves among other things a particular use of language theology is, whether the fact be acknowledged by theologians or not, vitally linked with the arts and the problems raised by artistic creativity. Hence the amount of space taken up in this book with discussion of the nature of religious language, and the use of symbol, myth and metaphor in religion.

These subjects are of common interest to theologians and students of literature, and of the arts in general. The question of theology and language is however of special concern to the *Christian* theologian and the reason for this has never been better expressed than by St Augustine. In a famous passage in his *De Trinitate* he discusses the question why Christians should use trinitarian language when speaking about God. He is aware of the irritation and impatience of those who feel that theological language is attempting to make definitions precisely in a sphere where, in the nature of the case, such a thing is not possible. Augustine replies, however, that Christians have to be careful about language, especially language about God, *non ut diceretur sed ne taceretur*, which could be paraphrased 'not in order to define but because it is not possible just to say nothing'. Christians, of all people, cannot keep silence, adds Augustine, because God has broken silence in Christ and has spoken to mankind in him. We are bound therefore to make the best reply that we can.

More particularly theology invites comparison with what may properly be called the art of criticism, since it has the same relation to its subject matter (religion) as, for example, music criticism has to the symphony, art criticism to painting or sculpture, or literary criticism to poetry or prose. The best theology, like the best art, is that which so uses language that it sends the reader back with new and fruitful perspectives to the original (e.g., Christ, the Bible, etc.), or so speaks of the original that it affords a fresh and creative present experience of it.

Perhaps because of the great variety of approaches and methods possible for doing theology it is better, and here again the analogy from art is useful, not to think of what theology may be in the abstract but of actual types and styles of theology, and it is hoped that the selections given in this book will enable the reader to do this. The types and styles of theology are analogous to the types and styles of art. One could readily think in theology of the equivalents of, say, representational, impressionist, expressionist or abstract art. The 'quest of the historical Jesus' in the nineteenth century bears a resemblance to the 'pre-Raphaelite' school of painting in its attempt to portray Jesus in full and minute detail. Rudolf Bultmann and the 'existentialist' school of modern theology remind one of German 'expressionist' art where the subject of the painting is used as a means of expressing the commitment, feeling and attitudes of the artist. Further, like styles in art, theological styles continue to have significance even though they belong to an age now long past. The artist and the theologian are both in constant dialogue with their past traditions. To be a genuine contemporary, in both fields, means to have lived through, in imaginative experience, the outlook of previous practitioners. Theology belongs to the realm of human creativity and is therefore a dynamic and changing phenomenon. It is better, therefore, at the beginning of one's study of such a subject to look at the various methods of doing theology rather than to seek some distillation of it, some quintessential theology.

It would not be difficult to say something about what theology is from an analysis of the two words which make up the term theology—'theos' and 'logos'. Starting from these two components we might translate 'theology' as 'God-talk'. Theology as 'God-talk' takes its origin from two permanent features of human existence. There is first the fact that from time to time, in all sorts of ways, man finds himself wondering whether there is any meaning to his existence, whether the values and ideals which strike him in a cogent way in his many moral and aesthetic experiences are anything more than fine moments of feeling. There is further an impatience and a restlessness about human existence—we long for serenity, for wholeness and harmony, for unity and purpose, and continue to wonder whether in and behind material existence there is another order of reality.

These intimations of something beyond time and space have been variously expressed whether in the classical scheme of the values of 'truth, beauty and goodness', or in what Rudolf

Otto[1] has called the experience of the 'holy' or the 'numinous', or as far as aesthetic experience is concerned, in what Longinus[2] called the 'sublime'. Others have used the term 'mystery' for these features of human existence to express their sense of that which is mysterious, not in the way of a puzzle which is in principle solvable at some time or other, but as inducing, rather than the desire to solve, an overwhelming impression of awe, wonder, reverence, joy.

For the centre of this 'mystery' the Greek word would have been *theos*, sometimes translated 'god', but we may conveniently use it for any kind of transcendental reference given to human life. Man is a being who finds it difficult to undergo artistic, religious, scientific or moral experience and leave it just like that. He finds himself involved necessarily in the task of shaping this experience into significant patterns, trying to hold it in words or in some visual form. More particularly he is prompted to speech about it, to try and contain this experience in sentences. It is to this necessary use of language to analyse and explain *theos* that one can give the Greek word *logos*. Theology is, therefore, strictly speaking *theos-logos*— 'God-talk'. Theology results from the fact that on the one hand there is the 'mystery' and on the other the impulse to achieve understanding of it.

It is significant that many theologians have expressed a similar impatience with their task to that which we find in poets. We have already referred to Augustine and T. S. Eliot on the difficulties and frustrations of finding satisfactory words. This raises an important issue. Most frequently when we use the term 'theology' we think, inevitably and rightly, of verbal theology: that analysis of the 'mystery' of existence, that articulation of *theos* which can be done in words (*logos*). No doubt one would have to say that the best theology is that which approximates most closely to the character of its subject-matter. In the case of Christian theology this would mean the character of the Incarnation especially its 'signful', indirect, ambiguous, parabolic quality. Perhaps a more adequate kind of theology, a more satisfactory response to the *theos*, is that

[1] *The Idea of the Holy*, 1923.

[2] Cassius Longinus, Greek philosopher and critic of third century A.D., author of a treatise on literary criticism, *On the sublime*.

expressed in a concrete but non-verbal way in the arts, particularly the visual arts. If this is the case we ought to coin a new word for this reaction to *theos*. It would be a question not of *theos* and *logos* (=*verbal* theology) but of *theos* and *poiesis* ('making')—'theo-poetics'. The use of such a term as 'theo-poetics' would remind one of the saying of W. B. Yeats, specially appropriate to the Christian religion, that man cannot know the truth or express it in words. He can only *embody* (perhaps one could say 'incarnate') it. Even if we must continue to use the word 'theology' we need to think of it as a perennial attempt to *embody* human experience of *theos* rather than to translate it into some prose paraphrase.

This analysis of the meaning of the word 'theology' is a start, but it does not take us very far. We need to examine more closely how theologians have set about the task of 'God-talk', and the data which they have taken to be relevant. We must therefore turn now to a brief review of what theologians have been doing during the last two centuries. This will help us to understand the theological scene today, and to recognize more clearly some of the 'styles' being used by theologians at the present time.

1

A radical change came over the method of doing Christian theology in the eighteenth century. Up till then, broadly speaking, and certainly from the time when theology had been given its most comprehensive and systematic expression in the works of St Thomas Aquinas (*c.* 1225–74) the procedure had seemed straightforward and uncomplicated. The scheme of theological investigation had two main parts: (1) natural theology and (2) revealed theology.

To take the method of doing 'natural' theology first. It was thought possible to establish by the ordinary processes of human reasoning such great truths as the existence of God and the immortality of the soul. Furthermore the ordinary processes of argumentation could establish the truth of certain attributes of God, like his omnipotence and omnipresence. From the evidence provided by the natural world and human existence it was possible to establish the existence of God by 'proofs'. The existence of God could be demonstrated by the use of unaided human reason. This was a truth about God open to any enquirer and could therefore rightly be called 'natural' theology.

'Revealed' theology was an important supplement to this. It had two additional functions to those performed by natural theology. First of all it conveyed again the truths of natural theology but this time in a 'revealed' form (particularly in the Christian scriptures) which could be readily and easily understood by those who were not able to follow rational argument. Then, second, revealed theology presented truths which could not be demonstrated by human reason, such as, for instance, the trinitarian nature of God. The scriptures attested the divinity of Christ by showing that he fulfilled Old Testament prophecy and worked miracles. These were taken to be the two foundations of belief in the authority of Christ. They established his place in the Christian revelation.

There were thus two kinds of data at the disposal of the theologian, natural theology and revealed theology, or to put it shortly 'reason' and 'revelation'. From an investigation of the book of nature and the book of scripture the theologian could construct an integrated and systematic theology, like the *Summa Theologiae* of St Thomas Aquinas. This was the general pattern of Christian apologetics commonly accepted until comparatively recently, and has remained the official view of the matter in the Roman Catholic Church. This method of doing theology was enshrined in William Paley's *View of the Evidences of Christianity* (1794) which remained in use as a text-book until as late as the beginning of the present century. Various criticisms had been brought against this way of doing theology before the advent of modern developments in philosophy, the sciences, and in biblical criticism. Reformation theology in general was suspicious of the large claims made by natural theology for the use of man's 'unaided' reason. Not only did the Reformers insist on the fact that all reasoning is undergirded by grace but they questioned whether one could say that human reason, even when so supported, inevitably attained the truths of natural theology. This seemed to them to neglect the problem of 'fallen' human nature which is capable of perverting and corrupting even the process of reasoning. During the eighteenth century the unsatisfactory character of this traditional approach to theology became clearer still. Many Christian apologists in this period tried to develop a natural theology not by reading off from the book of nature but by searching, so to speak, the book of man's inner experience. This seemed to show that there was among human beings a general religious sense which lay behind all formally organized religions. So-called 'revealed' theology was therefore taken to be simply a sophisticated articulation of this universal natural theology. In this way the distinction between natural and revealed theology was blurred, to say the least. Christianity, for example, was seen not as a blend of natural and revealed theology but a particular version of the universal feeling for religion. To quote from the title of a book by a famous eighteenth-century Deist, Matthew Tindal, it was as 'old as creation', nothing more than 'a republication of the religion of nature'.

More dramatic in their effects on the traditional scheme of theology, however, were the developments in scientific investigation and historical criticism which gathered momentum during the eighteenth century and continued apace throughout the nineteenth century.

2

Research in the natural sciences during the nineteenth century, especially in the fields of geology and biology, produced a picture of the origin of the universe and its evolution radically different from that suggested by a literal acceptance of the early chapters of Genesis with a universe created in six days and an Adam and Eve as the first human beings. *The Bridgewater Treatises* (1833–40) showed, among other things, that it was quite impossible, from the evidence already made available by geological research, to subscribe to the view that Creation could be exactly dated, as Archbishop Ussher[1] had

1 James Ussher (1581–1656), Archbishop of Armagh, worked out a complete biblical chronology in his *Annales Veteris et Novi Testamenti*, and the dates given in this book were inserted in editions of the Authorised Version of the Bible from 1701 onwards.

suggested, in 4004 B.C. For those who had been brought up on the idea that the Bible was itself the revelation of God, giving infallible truth as a series of propositions, this suggestion that the earth was millions rather than thousands of years old came as quite a shock. As late as 1851 John Ruskin could write: 'If only the geologists would let me alone, I could do very well, but those dreadful hammers! I hear the clink of them at the end of every cadence of the Bible verses.'

Following hard upon this shock came the news from the field of biological research. Charles Darwin's *The Origin of Species* was published in 1859 and his *The Descent of Man* in 1871. These made it clear not only that human life had evolved from sub-human species but that the whole process had been inconceivably longer than was generally supposed. Again for those brought up on the view that the Bible was a monolithic structure infallible on all subjects, including the science of human origins, this came as a great blow.

These shocks from outside the sphere of the Bible coincided with developments within biblical criticism which at the time seemed to undermine still further the status of the Bible as authoritative Scripture. As a result of literary and historical study it was no longer possible to maintain that the biblical literature was all of one kind, and all on the same level of authority or 'inspiration'. To take the Bible as an infallible oracle, to believe that in it the Word of God took print, was now seen to violate the nature of the biblical literature itself and to presuppose that the divine method of revelation is one which imposes rather than elicits, 'explains' rather than indicates, and forces rather than persuades.

Faced with these developments there were three possible reactions from Christian apologists. One could first simply refuse to recognize that any change had taken place and to carry on using the Bible as before, if anything hardening one's ideas about its authority and inerrancy. This is the approach which later on came to have the label 'fundamentalism' attached to it. Or, secondly, the attempt could be made to reconcile the new developments in knowledge with the traditional structure of theology. This was often taken to quite fantastic lengths like, for example, suggesting that the real significance of fossils in no way turned out to be a contradiction of the traditional dating of creation since they had been placed there by God to test faith! Similarly one remembers the notorious attempts to reconcile evolution with the scheme of creation in Genesis. Since the psalmist says that one day in the sight of the Lord is as a thousand years, 'days' in the Genesis account does not mean twenty-four hours but whatever extended period of time may be necessary to fit the case! Or, thirdly, one could accept the findings of research and in the light of them discard previous views of, for example, biblical inerrancy and look entirely afresh at the whole concept of revelation and the nature of the biblical literature. It was this latter reaction that has come to be known as nineteenth-century liberalism. Its main features were as follows.

First, a suspicion of the traditional schemes of dogmatic theology, and an attempt to reconstruct Christian belief in a way which took into account historical criticism. This could be illustrated by new procedures in such areas as christology or the doctrine of the Church. The traditional belief about the Christ as true God and true man, with two natures divine and human, as expressed in the traditional formula of the Council of Chalcedon 451 was put on one side, and an attempt made to construct a way of believing in Christ taking into account the results of historical criticism of the gospels, particularly the growing conviction that the fourth gospel, which had been a principal source for the formulation of traditional christology, was so much later than the synoptic gospels and so much less historical that it ought not to be used again in this way. The enigmatical Christ of the synoptic gospels, only indirectly indicating the meaning of himself, became the basis for a 'kenotic' christology. That is to say it was emphasized that whatever else the Incarnation was it meant an act of self-giving on the part of God which involved sacrificial self-limitation. Or again one could take the doctrine of the Church, especially in its relation to Christ. In the light of biblical and historical criticism it was felt by many nineteenth-century scholars that the Christ of history, the genuine Jesus of Nazareth, was one thing, and the Christ of Church doctrine quite another. It seemed to be self-evident that the historical Christ could not have intended the Church as an institution, but rather that he was an outstanding Hebrew prophet who was concerned with brotherly love, justice, and the inestimable worth of the human soul.

The second characteristic of nineteenth-century liberalism was the use made of the category of evolution, provided by developments in the biological sciences. Human history was seen in terms of evolutionary progress. Mankind was seen to be, indubitably, on the march of progress. By the use of reason and the intellectual tools at his disposal man would be able to fashion a better future for himself. 'Sin', if the word were used at all, ought to be put in inverted commas and translated to mean imperfection or ignorance. 'Salvation' consequently ought to be thought of in terms of education and enlightenment. Such biblical concepts as 'the kingdom of God' ought similarly to be reinterpreted in terms of some kind of evolutionary progressivism.

Out of all this came some new principles for theological method and the data to be used by theology. The Bible remained as a principal source for the Christian theologian but it had to be used critically in the light of the findings of literary and historical investigation. The Bible also needed to be detached from its traditional interpretation in the church. In particular allegorization and typology were discarded as both inappropriate and irrelevant to such a critical use of the Bible. The book of the universe, nature, was also a source to be used, especially since it provided such a category of interpretation as evolutionary development. Finally there was increasing use of human experience as a source for theology. Nineteenth-century theology was greatly influenced by the work of Friedrich Schleiermacher (1768–1834) who considered the essence of the religious sentiment to be the feeling of absolute dependence and interpreted Christ as the supreme example of such dependence and 'God-consciousness'.

As far as relations with philosophy were concerned it has to be remembered that in the nineteenth century the task of philosophy was taken to be, principally, to provide a 'metaphysics', that is an all-embracing interpretation of the universe and human existence. The philosopher was one who concerned himself with what Tillich (see Vol. 3, pp. 73 ff.) called the 'ultimate questions of human existence'. The theologian's task was to keep on the look-out for philosophical schemes whose general outlook and vocabulary seemed to be particularly well-suited for the exposition of Christian beliefs. It was widely held during the nineteenth century, both on the Continent and in Britain, that such a congenial philosophical system had been found in the work of Friedrich Hegel (1770–1831). Hegel believed that existence could best be interpreted in terms of an evolutionary process, continually advancing from thesis to antithesis and fresh sythesis, whereby the Absolute Idea realized itself in ever more sharply focused ways. Adapting Christian trinitarian language he thought of the eternal Idea as God the Father. The eternal Idea as constantly passing from infinitude to finitude he thought of as God the Son. The Absolute Idea returning home, so to speak, enriched by this outgoing (Incarnation) he identified with the Christian God the Holy Spirit.

3

This was the background against which we can place all the theological movements represented in this series. Paul Tillich has described himself as a nineteenth-century figure, and certainly his concept of the relation between theology and philosophy as a 'correlation' (see Vol. 3, pp. 39 ff.) makes him very much more akin to the philosophy of the last century than to the analytical anti-metaphysical philosophy which has dominated the academic scene in twentieth-century Britain. Karl Barth's theological thinking began as a strong reaction against the liberal theology of the nineteenth-century and particularly its alliance with philosophies which he believed prevented the unique and distinctive features of the Christian religion from being clearly expressed. Bultmann took up the issues raised by the development of biblical criticism in the nineteenth century, particularly the question of the relation between the Jesus of history and the Christ of faith. Bonhoeffer in his early period shared Barth's reaction to nineteenth-century theology but later came to believe that a quite new situation faces the twentieth-century Christian and that Barth was of decreasing usefulness to such a person. Niebuhr's theology of politics and society is a deliberate reaction to a liberal theology which he believed had seriously underplayed the doctrines of sin and original sin and had placed an ultimate trust in human intelligence and virtue. We now need to examine more fully the place in the history of twentieth-century theology likely to be occupied by these five theologians.

All five of them were German or, in the case of Niebuhr, of German origin. As it happens they were also all of clerical or academic households. Further they all had experienced the age of Nazism and in most cases had suffered from it in one way or another.

The beginning of the theological movement associated with the name of *Karl Barth* can be dated from his shocked realization that the values of nineteenth-century liberalism as held by academics and intellectuals of his day left them incapable of recognizing tyranny when it appeared, much less of standing up against it. Academic education, even in theology, did not make men any more able to perceive the illiberalism and aggression implicit in the German policies which led to the outbreak of the 1914–18 war (see Vol. 1, pp. 36 ff.). The same inability of the liberal mind to believe in the recalcitrant and anti-rational possibilities of human conduct displayed itself again when the Nazis came to power in 1934. The theological charter which became the rallying point of church resistance to Hitler, the Barmen declaration, was mainly the work of Barth.

Certainly nothing could be more contrary to the theological method of nineteenth-century liberalism than that promulgated by Barth. For him the theological endeavour begins not with a series of questionings about human existence or the universe but by a realization that man is first confronted by an answer, a divine answer in the form of a revelation to which a unique witness is borne by the Bible. 'Religion' as the human enquiry after God, the human endeavour to attain God by the exercise of human reason is anathema to Barth (see Vol. 1, pp. 56 ff.). It is impossible for man to take any initiative, strictly speaking, in his enquiries about God because by his very existence man is a potential recipient of a revelation which is one of the inescapable givennesses of life. God is essentially a prevenient God who has first spoken to man, and anything that man says, any enquiry that he may make, must necessarily take the form of a response to a God who has all the while been addressing him. This is a method of doing theology directly opposed to that of Paul Tillich who begins his theology precisely with human questions, the 'ultimate questions' posed by human existence.

This starting point led Barth to place a new kind of emphasis on the Bible and the place of scripture in the formation of dogmatic theology. This started a movement which later on came to be known as 'biblical theology'. The Bible was regarded as providing the categories for Christian theology. Barth's theology has been given different names. One of them, his own term, is 'kerygmatic' theology, namely a theology which has first and foremost to be proclaimed. It is not sensible to argue about revelation Barth believed; one can only proclaim it.

There is also in Barth a new emphasis on the indissoluble links between theology and the church. Academic theology in the nineteeth century, especially in Germany, was separated from the life of the Church and the work of the pastor. The Church as the believing community came to have a new meaning for Barth as the body which finds itself bearing the Word of God and being judged by it.

Barth's way of doing Christology, of tackling the problems raised by the person of Christ, seems at first sight to be very much in the traditional manner. He began from the traditional formulation of the Council of Chalcedon of Christ as true God and true man. But he soon showed himself to be suspicious of the historical method of the nineteenth-century 'quest of the historical Jesus'. Barth suspected that this really made faith dependent on the results of historical investigation and practically equivalent to acceptance of an agreed amount of reliable factual information about Christ. It is instructive at this point to compare Barth's attitude to the historical Jesus with that of Bultmann, Tillich and Bonhoeffer. Barth treated more creatively and fruitfully than the nineteenth century the question of *kenosis* (self-emptying) in the Incarnation. This was not for Barth a matter of some loss of divinity, a downgrading of God. The *kenosis* in Christ is in fact the highest affirmation of the lordship of God over all. God is lord not only in transcendent glory but even in the form of the servant. God is free to be other personalities without ceasing to be himself. Whereas for so many 'kenotic' theologians in the nineteenth (and indeed twentieth centuries) the Incarnation had meant God revealing himself in a very qualified and impoverished way, for Barth the Incarnation is the expression (the Word) of a God who always had man, and the glorification on man, in mind. God in Christ revealed his majesty precisely in the humiliations, trials and sufferings of Christ which many theologians in the past had thought must conceal it.

The resulting shape of Barth's theological scheme gives central place to the Incarnation, Scripture, and the Church. All Christian theology turns out in the end, according to Barth, to be an aspect of Christology whether it be the doctrine of creation, or of the church, or of the sacraments.[1]

Barth may have been neo-Calvinist in his approach to the doctrine of man, emphasizing human impotence before God, but in the end his theology of man turns out to be more optimistic than, say, that of Tillich or Niebuhr. There is a warm glow about Barth's language when he writes about man as he is in Christ, re-created man. On the other hand his theology is distanced from cultural and social interests. Barth saw what he called a *diastasis,* a tension between theology and the arts where Tillich perceived the possibilities of 'correlation'.

For *Bultmann* too the 1914–18 war was a turning point. It was during this period that he was working as a New Testament scholar on the form-critical method (see Vol. 2, pp. 37 ff.) and this proved to be determinative for his later work. He was sceptical about being able to get behind the 'kerygmatic' Christ of the gospels and sure that we do not have data for providing informed discussion about such subjects as the motivation of Christ or the self-awareness about his own mission. As well as the influence of Bultmann's scholarly investigations we need to reckon with his deep interest in the problem of communication, and his concern with the pastoral problems created by the fact that the tradition about Jesus comes down to us in a 'mythological' form. The extent of this problem was brought home to him by what he heard from army chaplains in the Second World War about their experiences in trying to preach and teach. This raised in an acute form the whole

[1] *Church Dogmatics*, I, 2, pp. 123 ff.

question of how the Christian gospel is to be communicated in the modern world. This involved a study of the status of 'mythology' in the Christian religion. Is it an essential form of human speech, or it is accidental, temporary, continually replaceable by more satisfactory translations or paraphrases into other kinds of language? Bultmann came to believe the latter and hence insisted upon the need for 'demythologizing' (see Vol. 2, pp. 64 ff.).

Bultmann took over the language of 'existentialist' philosophy as that which is specially well equipped to express the kind of religious belief we find in the New Testament. 'Existentialist' thinking is that in which we are ourselves personally involved, the kind of thinking in which we are personally implicated. It calls for personal decision and genuine commitment. Existentialism is antipathetic to any philosophy which is merely theoretical or academic (in the bad sense). The debate started by Bultmann's transposition of New Testament belief into existentialist terms has centred on whether this emphasis on the subjective, on *my* decision and commitment here and now, is adequate to do justice to the many facets of Christianity. Is not the New Testament also concerned with certain objective facts, like the redemption wrought by Christ, which remain true irrespective of any personal decision and commitment. Sometimes after reading a lot of Bultmann one has the feeling that when the existentialist theologian says 'God' he really means 'me'. Or at least it sounds like that!

Bultmann shares the hesitations of Barth about exposing the Incarnation to the ambiguities and probabilities of historical investigation. This would make faith vulnerable to the hazards of historical criticism and Bultmann, like Barth, seems intent on finding some area for faith which is immune from that eventuality.

So the data for theology which is to determine one's starting point is not the world, nor is it the Bible in the way Barth takes it, although the New Testament plays a cardinal role in Bultmann's theology. Rather it is human existence, because this is where the whole question of faith is posed. The mythological idiom of the New Testament really relates to man in his existential predicaments, to the need for decision, and for turning from 'inauthentic' to 'authentic' existence.

When we turn to *Paul Tillich* we find a theologian who is very much closer than Barth or Bultmann to the liberal tradition and to principles of liberal investigation. Tillich's whole approach to theology is based on the assumption that man has a natural ability to apprehend truth and that there is in man 'a depth of reason'. He starts from anthropology, examining the implications of the questions which are set by human existence.

Tillich agreed with Barth that theology is 'kerygmatic' but he insisted that it is also 'apologetic'. He kept a place for 'natural theology'. If theology is treated as only 'kerygmatic' Tillich believed, and I think rightly, that it then becomes irrelevant outside the domestic circle of believers, and is only useful for 'revivalism', as he put it.

Tillich departed radically from Bultmann on the question of myth and symbol. 'Demythologizing' for Tillich was an impossible enterprise because the myth is by its very nature irreplaceable and untranslatable, and cannot be transposed into a paraphrase without serious distortion or reduction. 'Myth' is a significant pattern of symbols organized into a narrative story which has the peculiar power, whenever it is receptively read or heard of bringing with it a clearer perception and deeper understanding of some feature of human experience which can not be evoked or expressed in any other way. Tillich believed that myth was therefore fundamentally irreplaceable. Bultmann on the other hand does not see myth existing in its own permanent right, but rather as a temporary way of putting things in a certain culture, which may now be seen perhaps as striking and picturesque, but not a necessary form of human speech.

Tillich was outstanding among the group represented in this series, and indeed in the twentieth century generally, for the attention he gave to analysing the relation between theology and culture. On this issue he was far removed from Barth and closer to a thinker like Niebuhr.

Reinhold Niebuhr's work can also be seen as a reaction against the preceding liberal theology. He is specially critical of the tendencies in nineteenth-century theology to equate the 'kingdom of God' with social betterment or progress. His theological endeavour could be described as an essay in 'prophetic

realism'. He sought, that is to say, to relate biblical insights
into the meaning of history and God's judgement on and in it
to the political and social situation of his day. His aim was
'realism' in the sense that he had a deep suspicion of what one
American writer has called 'the men of the infinite', that is the
idealists, the romantics, the men of abstract generalization.
Niebuhr preferred the company of 'the men of the finite', those
with a careful eye for data, evidence, facts. A good example of
this 'prophetic realism' is to be found in the essay 'The
ultimate trust' in *Beyond Tragedy*.

Like Tillich, but unlike Barth, Niebuhr starts from the
human situation. Here again one finds his work a marked
contrast to nineteenth-century liberalism in the way he ex-
pounds afresh the doctrines of the 'fall of man' and 'original
sin', and the place he gives to eschatology. The basic form of
sin for Niebuhr is not finitude or imperfection but the anxiety
about them which human freedom makes possible and which
expresses itself in pride and envy.

Niebuhr takes up from liberal theology the results of biblical
criticism, especially as it affects biblical history. 'Funda-
mentalist' approaches to the Bible blurred the distinction
between different literary forms, and, most disastrously,
between symbolic language and language of historical fact.

The theology of *Bonhoeffer*, fragmentary though it be, is of
the greatest importance in showing a man struggling to free
himself from various traditions in his early training notably the
influence of Karl Barth, and re-cast the whole structure of
theology to face a new situation. Bonhoeffer came to believe
that the theology of Barth and Bultmann had seriously
neglected the social and political problems of the world. In
this respect he found the theology of Niebuhr, which he came
to know well as a result of his visits to America, very much
more congenial.

Bonhoeffer was very much concerned with the significance
of Christ, and especially the place of the historical Christ in
Christian belief. His theology is, in one respect, an attempt to
reconstruct a Christocentric theology and ethics just as
thoroughgoing in its Christocentricity as Barth's. He does not,
however, isolate the place and role of the Bible in the manner

of Barth nor does he put the whole stress on inwardness in the existentialist fashion of Bultmann and Tillich.

4

The theologians represented in this series are already established figures on the twentieth-century theological scene, and their writings have by now attained the status of 'classics'. What developments have there been among a younger genera- of theologians? Recently a number of new movements have come into vogue which could be given the labels: 'The new theology', 'Secular Christianity' and 'The death of God theology'. There is space here only for a brief word about each of these developments.

One of the most astonishing phenomena in recent years has been the popular success of Dr John A. T. Robinson's *Honest to God*, first published in 1963, which has now sold well over one million copies, as well as being translated into a great number of foreign languages. The extraordinary circulation of this book is strange because it was not written for a popular audience, it contains long extracts from Tillich, Bultmann and Bonhoeffer which make severe demands on the general reader, and it could not be described as a piece of creative or lucid theological writing. The author would be the first to say that he was not attempting a new theology but to promote a discussion of the three thinkers just mentioned who had hitherto, especially in this country, been known only by academics and professional theologians. It was perhaps the tone of voice of this book rather than its contents which gave it such popular appeal particularly since the author was a bishop, with all that the image of such a person still implies in this country. The picture which the book suggested of a bishop not pontificating theological certainties in dogmatizing fashion, but exploring in a very tentative way and voicing his own doubts and uncertainties, struck a new note for many people. *Honest to God* appeared to be the manifesto of a movement of liberation, and to express the feeling that belief was a continuous dialogue with doubt within each person, and not an unchangeable certainty over against the unbelief of others.

Many critics have pointed out the obscurities and confusions in Dr Robinson's book. One of these is significant and worth pausing over. This is the question of the place and function of metaphor in religious language which he brings up in the first chapter on the God 'up there or out there'. He expresses his irritation with this kind of language but without making it at all clear what he takes a phrase like 'God is up there' to mean. If he is arguing that God is not 'up there' in the sense that God is not an entity that one could theoretically examine in, say, the course of space exploration, this is an assertion not to be found in traditional Christian theology. There is, however, a sense in which it is most true to say that God is 'up there' or 'out there' and that is that 'God' is not simply another word for human life or experience at its most profound or intense. It is not clear, on this basic issue, which of the two uses the bishop has in mind.

This is a very significant area of confusion and it pinpoints what is a real situation of crisis in contemporary theology. This is 'the crisis of metaphor', and it bears on the discussions about 'myth' and symbolism to be found in a number of the extracts given in this series. Man as a finite being is bound to be a metaphor-making animal so long as he experiences intimations of realities outside or beyond what can be measured scientifically. This means, at the least, so long as he remains capable of aesthetic, moral, and mystical experience. The fact, for instance, that to indicate these experiences he uses the spatial language of a 'three-decker' universe ('up there', 'down there') is not the 'scandal' that Bultmann and Dr Robinson take it to be. This is a serious misplacing of what is the real 'stumbling-block' for twentieth-century man as far as Christian language is concerned. In fact the 'three-decker' universe is not a bad image to use in any talk about values and religious beliefs, at least for finite man in a space-time universe which is likely to be the condition of most of mankind in the foreseeable future. For spaceless man no doubt another image would be necessary, but until it is demonstrated that spaceless-ness is to be the permanent human state to try and dispense with spatial or temporal metaphor or even to be coy about its use is not a sign of maturity or progress. It indicates an inhuman and senseless attempt to try and jump out of our finite skin. The momentum of the human mind, as the poet Wallace Stevens put it, is towards abstraction. Part of the appeal of a 'demythologized' version of Christianity, suggested by Bultmann and others, and commended by Dr Robinson, is that it takes one away from the trying particularities of the concrete. But 'concretization', to use Bonhoeffer's term, is a necessary undertaking for the Christian religion as long as it is firmly rooted in an historical and particular Incarnation. It is this feature of the Christian religion which indicates where the real 'stumbling-block' for modern man has to be placed. This is precisely where St Paul put it, in the enigmatical ambiguity of a Christ who is so identified with the human scene as to be, seemingly, indistinguishable from it, except to the eyes of faith.

It would be generally true to say that all the theologians represented in this series took a view about the task of philosophy which has now become very unfashionable in Britain. They believed the job of the philosopher was to build up a world-view, a 'metaphysics'. Both Barth and Tillich shared this view. Barth suspected that the very 'world-view' inherent in philosophy would blur the distinctiveness of Christianity. Bultmann believed that 'existentialism' provided a coherent 'metaphysics' of human existence. Niebuhr and the earlier Bonhoeffer approached philosophy in the same way.

It is the special interest of Paul van Buren's *The Secular Meaning of the Gospel* (1963) that it discusses the relation between Christian theology and the type of linguistic or analytical philosophy which has developed in Britain and the United States. For philosophers like Ludwig Wittgenstein, G. E. Moore and A. J. Ayer the task of the philosopher is not to construct a 'world view' but to analyse and classify language. The philosopher studies how language works and the meanings which we attach to statements. He seeks to establish ways of verifying the truth of the various assertions we make.

In the first wave of linguistic analysis popularized by A. J. Ayer's *Language, Truth and Logic* (1936) it was asserted that the only kind of language which had meaning was that which was scientifically verifiable. All other types of language, poetry, for example, or moral exhortation or religion, were said to be meaningless because they were not susceptible to this kind of verification. Philosophical linguistic analysis has modified this position in recent years, and the concern now is how to classify the uses of language and to discuss the types of meaning appropriate to each in relation to the contexts in which they are used.

Paul van Buren seeks to relate the exposition of Christian theology to this kind of linguistic philosophical analysis. Also he has in mind the wish expressed by Bonhoeffer that one ought to be seeking for a 'non-religious interpretation' of biblical and theological concepts. van Buren's book has been nicknamed 'The case of the disappearing gospel'. Certainly in the process of re-stating Christianity in 'non-religious' language he so dissolves traditional Christian theology that it is difficult to see what if anything a believer of former times would recognize in it as familiar.

In *The Secular Meaning of the Gospel* van Buren contended that there is a residual Christianity, even when one has abandoned the idea that any meaning can be attached to 'God' or the 'transcendent'. This remainder he turns into a kind of moral heroism. Christ becomes for all men a model, *the* paradigm, of 'openness' and freedom. The significance of Christ is that he has shown himself, and continues to show himself to be a potent example of these qualities.

The most recent phase of theology has been called the 'death of God' movement. This is the title of a book by Gabriel Vahanian, and it has been used to describe the work not only of Vahanian but of Thomas Altizer (*The Gospel of Christian Atheism*) and William Hamilton, *The Essence of Christianity*.

If one complained about confusion in *Honest to God* this complaint would have to be brought even more sharply against some of these theologians, especially Altizer, whose work is irritatingly rhapsodic just at the points where clarity of expression is most required. It is not at all easy to be sure of what exactly is being said. In one way Altizer seems to be saying that Nietzsche's cry, 'God is dead', still needs repeating, particularly since as far as modern man in a technological society is concerned belief in God as a transcendent reality upon whom mankind depends has no meaning, and is hopelessly irrelevant. Man must now look to his own resources as he prepares to take charge of his own evolution.

Another side of Altizer seems to be saying, again in a very

confused way, that Christians have been reluctant to come to realistic terms with the Incarnation, particularly with its corollary that Christ really died the death. This is a useful point because it is true that Christians have traditionally not only denied that Christ was born in the way that we are, but there remained for a long time in Christian theology, especially in the Greek church, the belief that Christ's human flesh was not mortal flesh as ours is.

Altizer wishes to press the reality of the *kenosis* or self-giving in Incarnation so that one can say with Charles Péguy, 'God too has faced death'. But Altizer seems to take *kenosis* to mean a literal self-annihilation. He speaks of the death of God as 'an historical event'. If these words mean anything Altizer is saying that in the Incarnation God, as it were, committed suicide. The death of God in Christ has freed us to become our own Christs, the result of the Incarnation being that God has diffused himself in the human race. This sounds like a new version of pantheism.

What is specially interesting in the 'death of God' theologians is the place which they are still willing to accord to Christ. In spite of form-criticism and the wave of scepticism which it produced both Altizer and Hamilton seem to believe that there is sufficiently reliable information available about Jesus to warrant our thinking again about the ideal of the 'imitation of Christ'. This is interpreted along very different lines from Bonhoeffer's presentation of the *imitatio Christi*. It reminds one of what Kierkegaard called 'admiration of Christ', a heroic endeavour to reproduce his 'openness' and 'freedom' by sheer effort of will.

5

It is hazardous to suggest what is likely to be the prospect for theology in the rest of this century. However, it seems to me that four areas will provide material for special clarification: (1) There is first what I have called the 'crisis of metaphor' in modern theology. Theology and religious language stand or fall by metaphor and all that it implies about human life and human perception. The impulse to metaphor, to speak of one

• •

thing in terms of another, prompts the question whether the relation between appearance and reality may not be of the kind which religious belief suggests. The surrender of metaphor means the end of religion and, significantly, the death of what we have come to regard as distinctively human feelings. The French 'anti-novelist' Alain Robbe-Grillet is perfectly right to detect an important link between metaphor and religion. Robbe-Grillet wishes to get rid of metaphor because it implies some hidden relationship between man and the universe, and this takes us half-way to religion. Indeed, there is a 'crisis of metaphor' in modern literature as well as in modern theology. Bultmann can speak disparagingly of 'mere metaphors' and advocates 'demythologization' because myth, metaphor and symbol can be taken in a crude literal way, or can become obsolete. These are certainly hazards in the human situation, which often necessitate a drastic process of unlearning. But a worse fate, a greater hurt to the soul is to attempt to bring about a state of affairs where such hazards are no longer possible. It is damaging either to identify metaphor and actuality or to romanticize pantheistically (in a way that alarms Robbe-Grillet), but it is worse to believe that as individuals and as a generation we have gone beyond the need for metaphor. At stake, therefore, in the present 'crisis of metaphor' in literature and religion is nothing less than the humanization or dehumanization of man.

(2) There needs to be very much more exploration of what Tillich called 'correlation' between religion and the arts. Christians have lived too long with the assumption that while art may have aesthetic or pedagogical value, it is no serious avenue to truth. Art has been regarded as useful for those who cannot read, and need pictures, but not for the literate who having mastered discursive reasoning and the manipulation of abstractions have no need of the image. Art has therefore been taken by many theologians to be inferior to philosophy, and on the whole Christian theologians have preferred to cultivate relations with philosophers rather than artists. This is, however, to beg the question whether art is a way of knowing which is as truth-bearing, in its way, as philosophical or scientific method. Christians have surrendered with amazing ease to the notion

that the image is a lesser form of truth than the concept, as if image and concept were simply alternative ways of saying the same thing, except that the image helps those who have more imagination than logic. It is arguable that the Christian religion would have gained as much (perhaps more) from association with art as it has from philosophy, not only for general apologetic reasons, but for intellectual arguments with what Schleiermacher called its 'cultural despisers'.

(3) Thirdly, there is the continuing work of interpreting afresh the significance of Christ and in the immediate future this will have to include a thorough exploration of what it means to talk about the uniqueness of Christ and his finality.

In spite of the central place which it occupies in the structure of their beliefs, it has proved persistently difficult for Christians to take the Incarnation with full realism and to follow through its implications in a rigorously realistic way. It took Christians a very long time indeed to accept the belief that the Incarnation meant taking a human biology exactly like ours. What a struggle there was in the early Church to get accepted the belief that Christ really died the death in the way that we do! The history of the iconography of the crucifixion in art shows that it took nearly five centuries before a body of Christ appeared on the cross, and then it is very much a live Christ who, eyes open, stands on the cross as a royal warrior looking through the scene. It took the Christian Church nearly ten centuries before a really dead body of Christ appeared on the cross, and even then it was not a death in suffering and agony. It is another century and a half before a bleeding, suffering emaciated Christ with a crown of thorns appears in the representation of the crucifixion. This is a long time, but it has taken Christians even longer to come anywhere near accepting that the Incarnation involved taking a genuine human psychology of the kind that might mean that Christ had to find his way to religious belief in exactly the same way as everybody else, through faith, through acting on signs which, because they are ambiguous and our freedom is real, can always be 'stumbling-blocks' ('scandals' in the New Testament) that offend. Just as dangerous as a theology based on the 'God of the gaps' has been a 'Christology of the gaps', that is, a tendency to insert a capacity for full divine self-awareness on the part of the historical Jesus in some 'gap' in his psyche, or, so it has sometimes been suggested, in his subconscious!

The question of the finality of Christ suggests the fourth area in which it is likely that theology will be specially engaged in the immediate future: comparative religion, and especially comparative theology.

(4) In the contemporary world it sometimes appears that the 'ecumenical' movement of unbelief grows faster than that of belief, so that all religions are finding themselves on the same side of the fence as far as faith that human life has a transcendental significance is concerned. In this situation there needs to be more conversation between the theologies of the religions, particularly those whose history gives them a special kinship: Judaism, Christianity and Islam. If the Christian has to start thinking again about the meaning of Incarnation and the unique place which he assigns to Christ there is no more bracing company in which he could explore this question than that of the Jew and Muslim.

The present-day student of the Christian doctrines of the Trinity and the Incarnation might well begin with reflection on the familiar strictures on these doctrines that come from the Jew and the Muslim: that they violate the concept of the unity of God, and, by involving God in human history in a finite way, blaspheme against the majesty of God. The Christian will want to have as rich a doctrine that God is one as the Jew or the Muslim, and that God is known in historical event, and perhaps this is now more likely to be attained by going to school theologically with these two religions. Further the three religions of Judaism, Christianity and Islam have much to give each other in working out afresh for our own day the meaning of what it is to be human. Bishop Kenneth Cragg has shown how profound a realization of the nature of man comes from relating the Jewish/Christian concept of man made in the 'image of God' to the Muslim concept of man as 'God's caliph'.[1]

Much needs to be unlearned and relearned in this field. Judaism, Islam and Buddhism have suffered from misleading propagandist slogans in the past like 'Jewish legalism', 'Islam

[1] Kenneth Cragg, *The Privilege of Man*, London, 1968.

is the most materialistic and least religious of the religions', 'Buddhism is insensitive to suffering or social justice'. These are Christian caricatures of the truth, and there is now a fresh chance, especially in those western countries which are now multi-religious, to rectify this distortion by mutual understanding in co-operative study.

BIOGRAPHICAL INTRODUCTION

Dietrich Bonhoeffer was born in 1906 in Breslau which was then in the German province of Silesia but is now, as a result of the last war, incorporated into Poland with the changed name of Wroclaw. There were eight in the family whose background was professional and academic. One brother was killed in the First World War and another, Klaus, executed by the Nazis a fortnight after Dietrich. The father whom Bonhoeffer spoke of as one of the great influences of his life was the first professor of psychiatry in the University of Berlin.

Bonhoeffer's family was not particularly religious. Eberhard Bethge, the friend and biographer of Bonhoeffer, speaks of 'the careful agnosticism of his father and brothers'. Bonhoeffer's own religious convictions, deep though they were, maintained maximum sensitivity to the difficulties and feelings of the unbeliever.

At the age of sixteen Bonhoeffer decided to study theology and entered the University of Berlin. Here he came under the influence of some of the great figures in German liberal protestant theology, among them Adolf von Harnack who impressed Bonhoeffer by his 'intellectual incorruptibility'. After graduation he became a lecturer in the University of Berlin.

The development of Bonhoeffer's mind and beliefs has been divided into three periods. In the first, covering roughly the years 1927–33, he was a student teacher in Berlin. During these years he might almost be said to have worked with the motto of the dramatist Berthold Brecht: 'the truth is concrete'. He was engaged on what Bethge calls the 'quest for the concrete nature of the message'. In other words he was becoming suspicious of the easy generalizations, idealisms, and romanticism of what an American writer has called 'the men of the infinite', those who theorize in terms of abstract principles, especially in ethics, with a careless disregard for facts, particular data and concrete situations. The theological method of Karl Barth, with its insistence on the concrete particularity of the historical Incarnation, greatly influenced Bonhoeffer at this time. He spent two weeks at a Seminar in Bonn conducted by Barth in the summer of 1931. This influence is to be seen in his doctoral thesis which was later to be published as *Sanctorum Communio*. Later on Bonhoeffer was to be more critical of what he called Barth's 'positivism in theology' (see p. 81).

The second formative period in Bonhoeffer's life extends from 1933–40 when he was working as a pastor in Germany and abroad. It was during this period that he published *The Cost of Discipleship* and *Life Together* which represent his early thinking about the character of a truly personal Christian life lived in community. These years also saw his first travels abroad. He was for a time an assistant chaplain at the German church in Barcelona and while there spent a year's leave of absence at the Union Theological Seminary in New York where Reinhold Niebuhr was Professor of Christian Ethics. In a report on this visit Bonhoeffer spoke of Niebuhr as 'one of the most significant and creative of contemporary American theologians' but missed in his work 'a doctrine of the person and redemptive work of Jesus Christ'. This first experience of America was to have a bracing and liberating effect on Bonhoeffer. It was a shock to be in an atmosphere where Germany was not the be-all and the end-all of things theological: 'they find German theology so utterly local, they simply don't understand it here; they laugh at Luther'. But it meant a broadening of his understanding of the problems of the re-union of Christian Churches, relations between Church and state, and race-relations.

This period of Bonhoeffer's life coincided with the rise of the Nazi movement in Germany and the outbreak of war. Bonhoeffer took his stand against the Nazis immediately. Two days after Hitler became chancellor of Germany Bonhoeffer was broadcasting an attack on the Nazi theory of leadership. The broadcast was interrupted. Disheartened by what he saw going on Bonhoeffer came to London as German pastor in charge of two churches. Here he developed further his interests in the ecumenical movement and began his friendship with Dr G. K. A. Bell, Bishop of Chichester. In 1934 came the Barmen Declaration (see Vol. 1, p. 38) and the formation of the German Confessional Church in opposition to the Nazi-sponsored 'German Christian' Church. Bonhoeffer unhesitatingly came down on the side of the Confessional Church. In 1935 he returned to Germany to take charge of an illegal body, the Confessing Church Seminary at Zingst on the Baltic. This seminary later moved to Finkelwaldt also on the Baltic coast, near Stettin. He started an experimental community, which he called the 'Bruderhaus', and his experience of this lay behind his book *Life Together*. The Bruderhaus Community was dissolved by the Nazis in 1937.

By this time Bonhoeffer was increasingly under the scrutiny of the Gestapo. Reinhold Niebuhr was very anxious to get him out of Germany and succeeded for a short time. Bonhoeffer paid his second visit to America in 1939 but when it appeared that war was inevitable he returned to Germany. He explained why in a letter to Niebuhr:

'Sitting here in Dr. Coffin's garden [1] I have had the time to think and to pray about my situation and that of my nation and to have God's will for me clarified. I have come to the conclusion that I have made a mistake in coming to America. I must live through this difficult period of our national history with the Christian people of Germany. I shall have no right to participate in the reconstruction of Christian life in Germany after the war if I do not share the trials of this time with my people. My brothers in the Confessing Synod wanted me to go. They may have been right in urging me to do so; but I was wrong in going. Such a decision each man must make for himself. Christians in Germany will face the terrible alternative of either willing the defeat of their nation in order that Christian civilisation may survive, or willing the victory of their nation and thereby destroying our civilisation. I know which of these alternatives I must choose; *but I cannot make that choice in security.*'

The final period of Bonhoeffer's life covers the years 1940–5, in which he became more and more involved in underground resistance activities. He continued with his writing, as opportunity offered, and it is in this last period that he began his most strenuous thinking about 'Christianity without religion in an adult world'.

[1] Principal of Union Theological Seminary.

In 1942 Bonhoeffer met Dr Bell, the Bishop of Chichester, this time in Stockholm, and he disclosed the plans to overthrow the Nazi regime. The following year he was arrested and imprisoned at Tegel, near Berlin, and it is to this period of captivity that the *Letters and Papers from Prison* belong. They were written to his friend Eberhard Bethge. Following the attempt on Hitler's life in July 1944 he was placed in close confinement in Berlin. Then he was sent to a number of concentration camps, including Buchenwald, and finally was hanged by the SS at Flossenbürg in Bavaria on 9 April 1945 shortly before it was liberated by the Americans.

SELECTIONS

1 'THE EMPIRICAL FORM OF THE CHURCH'

[Bonhoeffer was much concerned with the ambiguous character of the Christian Church. From one point of view it is a religious institution, and sociology can help to analyse and classify the characteristics of such an institution. On the other hand the Church is the 'Body of Christ', the organ of his presence in the world. The Christian religion for Bonhoeffer could never be thought of as a vague mysticism. A real visible historical Incarnation meant taking seriously and realistically the 'real presence' of Christ in his Church.]

(a) The objective spirit of the Church and the Holy Spirit
The Church of Jesus Christ actualized by the Holy Spirit is at the present moment really the Church. The communion of saints represented by it is 'in the midst of us'. This proposition gives rise to a twofold question about the empirical Church. There is the question of 'history and the communion of saints', and the question of the *communio peccatorum* within the *sanctorum communio*.[1]

The empirical Church is the organized 'institution' of salvation, having as its focus the cultus with preaching and sacrament, or, in sociological terms, the 'assembly' of the members. It is legally constituted, and links the bestowal of its benefits with the orders of divine service it lays down. It accepts all who submit to these orders, and hence has no guarantee for the inner disposition of its members, but, from the moment it is sanctioned by public opinion and perhaps has even become a political power in the state, it must necessarily reckon with the fact that it will have 'dead members' within it. It is the 'historical result of the work of Jesus Christ' (Seeberg), and as such represents the objective spirit of the Church in its development and being, in transmitted forms and embodiments and in present vitality and effectiveness. The objective spirit, as we saw, is the new spiritual principle springing from

[1] 'Community of sinners'; 'community of saints'. (Ed.)

socialization. The autonomous effectiveness of its will regulates and guides the wills of those partaking of and forming it. It is embodied in certain forms and thereby visibly authenticates its own life. Again, it acts in two directions, that is, it has an intention both in time and in space; it seeks to be effective both in the historical and in the social sphere. It is the bearer of historical tradition, and its action and effects are to include more and more individuals in its scope. It seems as if this sociological structure in the empirical Church should now be studied and analysed as presenting the religious type of community among many types of community. And yet if we did this we should entirely distort the matter. The empirical Church is not identical with a religious community. Rather, as a concrete historical community, in spite of the relativity of its forms, its imperfect and unpretentious appearance, the empirical Church is the Body of Christ, the presence of Christ on earth, for it has his Word. It is possible to understand the empirical Church only by looking down from above, or by looking out from the inside, and not otherwise. Once this fact has been grasped it is of course in principle possible once more to define the Church as a religious community, always bearing in mind that it is really based on God. Thus if we now apply to the Church what we said about the objective spirit, we have the claim of the objective spirit of the Church to be the bearer of the historical work of Jesus Christ and of the social action of the Holy Spirit.

The historical Church claims that it possesses the Holy Spirit and is the effective custodian of the Word of God and of the sacrament. This brings us to the first question, the great body of thought on the problem of the relation of the Spirit of Christ and the Holy Spirit of the *sanctorum communio* to the objective spirit of the empirical Church.

The *sanctorum communio* moved by the Holy Spirit has continually to be actualized in a struggle against two sources of resistance: human imperfection and sin. To equate the two, giving imperfection the weight of sin, or evaluating sin merely as imperfection, is to avoid the seriousness of the Christian concept of sin, and leads either to regarding the Church's sociologically empirical form as sin, or, in the manner of Kant, to viewing the empirical Church only as a manifestation of the non-real, ideal Church of the future or as unattainable in this world. Neither attitude does justice to the empirical Church's historical importance. The first is wrong because Christ entered into history so that the Church is his presence in history. The history of the Church is the hidden centre of world history, and not the history of one educational institution among many. For the Church is Christ existing as the Church. No matter how dubious its empirical form may be, it remains the Church so long as Christ is present in his Word. Thereby we acknowledge that God has willed the Church's historical life, in the sense that it is intended to perfect itself. The Body of Christ is just as much a real presence in history as it is the standard for its own history. This brings us once again to what was said at the beginning of our inquiry, about the normative character of basic ontic[1] relationships. In the sphere of Christian ethics it is not what ought to be that effects what is, but what is effects what ought to be.

(FROM : *Sanctorum Communio*, pp. 144–6.)

2 'CHEAP AND COSTLY GRACE'

[By 'cheap grace' Bonhoeffer meant a merely theoretical acceptance of Christianity, fluent no doubt in its verbal expression, but having no real awareness of the personal commitment, obedience and discipline involved. It is possible, for example, to pay all the correct lip-service to the Christian doctrine of redemption in such a way as to remain insensitive to the problems raised by human suffering and injustice. Bonhoeffer pays tribute to monasticism as an attempt to 'follow' Christ but criticizes it for becoming a way of salvation *from* the world, rather than *in* and *for* it. Luther he praises for restoring the belief that the imitation of Christ is not a man-made endeavour to copy Christ but a letting oneself be lived through by the Spirit of God who 'conforms' human beings to the likeness of Christ.]

[1] Basic relationships of being. (Ed.)

Cheap grace is the deadly enemy of our Church. We are fighting today for costly grace.

Cheap grace means grace sold on the market like cheap-jack's wares. The sacraments, the forgiveness of sin, and the consolations of religion are thrown away at cut prices. Grace is represented as the Church's inexhaustable treasury, from which she showers blessings with generous hands, without asking questions or fixing limits. Grace without price; grace without cost! The essence of grace, we suppose, is that the account has been paid in advance; and, because it has been paid, everything can be had for nothing. Since the cost was infinite, the possibilities of using and spending it are infinite. What would grace be if it were not cheap?

Cheap grace means grace as a doctrine, a principle, a system. It means forgiveness of sins proclaimed as a general truth, the love of God taught as the Christian 'conception' of God. An intellectual assent to that idea is held to be of itself sufficient to secure remission of sins. The Church which holds the correct doctrine of grace has, it is supposed, *ipso facto* a part in that grace. In such a Church the world finds a cheap covering for its sins; no contrition is required, still less any real desire to be delivered from sin. Cheap grace therefore amounts to a denial of the living Word of God, in fact, a denial of the Incarnation of the Word of God.

Cheap grace means the justification of sin without the justification of the sinner. Grace alone does everything, they say, and so everything can remain as it was before. 'All for sin could not atone.' The world goes on in the same old way, and we are still sinners 'even in the best life' as Luther said. Well, then, let the Christian live like the rest of the world, let him model himself on the world's standards in every sphere of life, and not presumptuously aspire to live a different life under grace from his old life under sin. That was the heresy of the enthusiasts, the Anabaptists[1] and their kind. Let the Christian beware of rebelling against the free and boundless grace of God and desecrating it. Let him not attempt to erect a new religion of the letter by endeavouring to live a life of

[1] The name given to a number of Protestant groups in the sixteenth century who emphasized 'believers baptism' rather than the baptism of infants. (Ed.)

obedience to the commandments of Jesus Christ! The world has been justified by grace. The Christian knows that and takes it seriously. He knows he must strive against this indispensable grace. Therefore—let him live like the rest of the world! Of course he would like to go and do something extraordinary, and it does demand a good deal of self-restraint to refrain from the attempt and content himself with living as the world lives. Yet it is imperative for the Christian to achieve renunciation, to practise self-effacement, to distinguish his life from the life of the world. He must let grace be grace indeed, otherwise he will destroy the world's faith in the free gift of grace. Let the Christian rest content with his worldliness and with this renunciation of any higher standard than the world. He is doing it for the sake of the world rather than for the sake of grace. Let him be comforted and rest assured in his possession of this grace—for grace alone does everything. Instead of following Christ, let the Christian enjoy the consolations of his grace! That is what we mean by cheap grace, the grace which amounts to the justification of sin without the justification of the repentant sinner who departs from sin and from whom sin departs. Cheap grace is not the kind of forgiveness of sin which frees us from the toils of sin. Cheap grace is the grace we bestow on ourselves.

Cheap grace is the preaching of forgiveness without requiring repentance, baptism without Church discipline, Communion without confession, absolution without personal confession. Cheap grace is grace without discipleship, grace without the cross, grace without Jesus Christ, living and incarnate.

Costly grace is the treasure hidden in the field; for the sake of it a man will gladly go and sell all that he has. It is the pearl of great price to buy which the merchant will sell all his goods. It is the kingly rule of Christ, for whose sake a man will pluck out the eye which causes him to stumble, it is the call of Jesus Christ at which the disciple leaves his nets and follows him.

Costly grace is the gospel which must be *sought* again and again, the gift which must be *asked* for, the door at which a man must *knock*.

Such grace is *costly* because it calls us to follow, and it *is grace* because it calls us to follow *Jesus Christ*. It is costly because it costs a man his life, and it is grace because it gives a man the only true life. It is costly because it condemns sin, and grace because it justifies the sinner. Above all, it is *costly* because it cost God the life of his Son: 'ye were bought at a price', and what has cost God much cannot be cheap for us. Above all, it is *grace* because God did not reckon his Son too dear a price to pay for our life, but delivered him up for us. Costly grace is the Incarnation of God.

Costly grace is the sanctuary of God; it has to be protected from the world, and not thrown to the dogs. It is therefore the living word, the Word of God, which he speaks as it pleases him. Costly grace confronts us as a gracious call to follow Jesus, it comes as a word of forgiveness to the broken spirit and the contrite heart. Grace is costly because it compels a man to submit to the yoke of Christ and follow him; it is grace because Jesus says: 'My yoke is easy and my burden is light.'

On two separate occasions Peter received the call, 'Follow me'. It was the first and last word Jesus spoke to his disciple (Mark 1:17; John 21:22). A whole life lies between these two calls. The first occasion was by the lake of Gennesareth, when Peter left his nets and his craft and followed Jesus at his word. The second occasion is when the Risen Lord finds him back again at his old trade. Once again it is by the lake of Gennesareth, and once again the call is: 'Follow me.' Between the two calls lay a whole life of discipleship in the following of Christ. Half-way between them comes Peter's confession, when he acknowledged Jesus as the Christ of God. Three times Peter hears the same proclamation that Christ is his Lord and God—at the beginning, at the end, and at Caesarea Philippi. Each time it is the same grace of Christ which calls to him 'Follow me' and which reveals itself to him in his confession of the Son of God. Three times on Peter's way did grace arrest him, the one grace proclaimed in three different ways.

This grace was certainly not self-bestowed. It was the grace of Christ himself, now prevailing upon the disciple to leave all and follow him, now working in him that confession which to the world must sound like the ultimate blasphemy, now inviting Peter to the supreme fellowship of martyrdom for the

Lord he had denied, and thereby forgiving him all his sins. In the life of Peter grace and discipleship are inseparable. He had received the grace which costs.

As Christianity spread, and the Church became more secularized, this realization of the costliness of grace gradually faded. The world was christianized, and grace became its common property. It was to be had at low cost. Yet the Church of Rome did not altogether lose the earlier vision. It is highly significant that the Church was astute enough to find room for the monastic movement, and to prevent it from lapsing into schism. Here on the outer fringe of the Church was a place where the older vision was kept alive. Here men still remembered that grace costs, that grace means following Christ. Here they left all they had for Christ's sake, and endeavoured daily to practise his rigorous commands. Thus monasticism became a living protest against the secularization of Christianity and the cheapening of grace. But the Church was wise enough to tolerate this protest, and to prevent it from developing to its logical conclusion. It thus succeeded in relativizing it, even using it in order to justify the secularization of its own life. Monasticism was represented as an individual achievement which the mass of the laity could not be expected to emulate. By thus limiting the application of the commandments of Jesus to a restricted group of specialists, the Church evolved the fatal conception of the double standard—a maximum and a minimum standard of Christian obedience. Whenever the Church was accused of being too secularized, it could always point to monasticism as an opportunity of living a higher life within the fold, and thus justify the other possibility of a lower standard of life for others. And so we get the paradoxical result that monasticism, whose mission was to preserve in the Church of Rome the primitive Christian realization of the costliness of grace, afforded conclusive justification for the secularization of the Church. By and large, the fatal error of monasticism lay not so much in its rigorism (though even here there was a good deal of misunderstanding of the precise content of the will of Jesus) as in the extent to which it departed from genuine Christianity by setting up itself as the individual achievement of a select few, and so claiming a special merit of its own.

When the Reformation came, the providence of God raised Martin Luther to restore the gospel of pure, costly grace. Luther passed through the cloister; he was a monk, and all this was part of the divine plan. Luther had left all to follow Christ on the path of absolute obedience. He had renounced the world in order to live the Christian life. He had learnt obedience to Christ and to his Church because only he who is obedient can believe. The call to the cloister demanded of Luther the complete surrender of his life. But God shattered all his hopes. He showed him through the Scriptures that the following of Christ is not the achievement or merit of a select few, but the divine command to all Christians without distinction. Monasticism had transformed the humble work of discipleship into the meritorious activity of the saints, and the self-renunciation of discipleship into the flagrant spiritual self-assertion of the 'religious'. The world had crept into the very heart of the monastic life, and was once more making havoc. The monk's attempt to flee from the world turned out to be a subtle form of love for the world. The bottom having thus been knocked out of the religious life, Luther laid hold upon grace. Just as the whole world of monasticism was crashing about him in ruins, he saw God in Christ stretching forth his hand to save. He grasped that hand in faith, believing that 'after all, nothing we can do is of any avail, however good a life we live'. The grace which gave itself to him was a costly grace, and it shattered his whole existence. Once more he must leave his nets and follow. The first time was when he entered the monastery, when he had left everything behind except his pious self. This time even that was taken from him. He obeyed the call, not through any merit of his own, but simply through the grace of God. Luther did not hear the word: 'Of course you have sinned, but now everything is forgiven, so you can stay as you are and enjoy the consolations of forgiveness.' No, Luther had to leave the cloister and go back to the world, not because the world in itself was good and holy, but because even the cloister was only a part of the world.

Luther's return from the cloister to the world was the worst blow the world had suffered since the days of early Christianity. The renunciation he made when he became a monk was child's play compared with that which he had to make when he returned to the world. Now came the frontal assault. The only way to follow Jesus was by living in the world. Hitherto the Christian life had been the achievement of a few choice spirits under the exceptionally favourable conditions of monasticism; now it is a duty laid on every Christian living in the world. The commandment of Jesus must be accorded perfect obedience in one's daily vocation of life. The conflict between the life of the Christian and the life of the world was thus thrown into the sharpest possible relief. It was a hand-to-hand conflict between the Christian and the world.

It is a fatal misunderstanding of Luther's action to suppose that his rediscovery of the gospel of pure grace offered a general dispensation from obedience to the command of Jesus, or that it was the great discovery of the Reformation that God's forgiving grace automatically conferred upon the world both righteousness and holiness. On the contrary, for Luther the Christian's worldly calling is sanctified only in so far as that calling registers the final radical protest against the world. Only in so far as the Christian's secular calling is exercised in the following of Jesus does it receive from the gospel new sanction and justification. It was not the justification of sin, but the justification of the sinner that drove Luther from the cloister back into the world. The grace he had received was costly grace. It was grace, for it was like water on parched ground, comfort in tribulation, freedom from the bondage of a self-chosen way, and forgiveness of all his sins. And it was costly, for, so far from dispensing him from good works, it meant that he must take the call to discipleship more seriously than ever before. It was grace because it cost so much, and it cost so much because it was grace. That was the secret of the gospel of the Reformation—the justification of the sinner.

Yet the outcome of the Reformation was the victory, not of Luther's perception of grace in all its purity and costliness, but of the vigilant religious instinct of man for the place where grace is to be obtained at the cheapest price. All that was needed was a subtle and almost imperceptible change of emphasis, and the damage was done. Luther had taught that man cannot stand before God, however religious his works and ways may be, because at bottom he is always seeking his own interests. In the depth of his misery, Luther had grasped by faith the free and unconditional forgiveness of all his sins. That experience taught him that this grace had cost him his very life, and must continue to cost him the same price day by day. So far from dispensing him from discipleship, this grace only made him a more earnest disciple. When he spoke of grace, Luther always implied as a corollary that it cost him his own life, the life which was now for the first time subjected to the absolute obedience of Christ. Only so could he speak of grace. Luther had said that grace alone can save; his followers took up his doctrine and repeated it word for word. But they left out its invariable corollary, the obligation of discipleship. There was no need for Luther always to mention that corollary explicitly for he always spoke as one who had been led by grace to the strictest following of Christ. Judged by the standard of Luther's doctrine, that of his followers was unassailable, and yet their orthodoxy spelt the end and destruction of the Reformation as the revelation on earth of the costly grace of God. The justification of the sinner in the world degenerated into the justification of sin and the world. Costly grace was turned into the cheap grace without discipleship.

Luther had said that all we can do is of no avail, however good a life we live. He had said that nothing can avail us in the sight of God but 'the grace and favour which confers the forgiveness of sin'. But he spoke as one who knew that at the very moment of his crisis he was called to leave all that he had a second time and follow Jesus. The recognition of grace was his final, radical breach with his besetting sin, but it was never the justification of that sin. By laying hold of God's forgiveness, he made the final, radical renunciation of a self-willed life, and this breach was such that it led inevitably to a serious following of Christ. He always looked upon it as the answer to a sum, but an answer which had been arrived at by God, not by man. But then his followers changed the 'answer' into the data for a calculation of their own. That was the root of the trouble. If grace is God's answer, the gift of Christian life, then we cannot for a moment dispense with following Christ. But if grace is the data for my Christian life, it means that I set out to live the Christian life in the world with all my sins justified beforehand. I can go and sin as much as I like, and rely on this grace to forgive me, for after all the world is justified in principle by grace. I can therefore cling to my bourgeois secular existence, and remain as I was before, but with the added assurance that the grace of God will cover me. It is under the influence of this kind of 'grace' that the world has been made 'Christian', but at the cost of secularizing the Christian religion as never before. The antithesis between the Christian life and the life of bourgeois respectability is at an end. The Christian life comes to mean nothing more than living in the world and as the world, in being no different from the world, in fact, in being prohibited from being different from the world for the sake of grace. The upshot of it all is that my only duty as a Christian is to leave the world for an hour or so on a Sunday morning and go to church to be assured that my sins are all forgiven. I need no longer try to follow Christ, for cheap grace, the bitterest foe of discipleship, which true discipleship must loathe and detest, has freed me from that. Grace as the data for our calculations means grace at the cheapest price, but grace as the answer to the sum means costly grace. It is terrifying to realize what use can be made of a genuine evangelical doctrine. In both cases we have the identical formula—'justification by faith alone'. Yet the misuse of the formula leads to the complete destruction of its very essence.

At the end of a life spent in the pursuit of knowledge Faust has to confess:

'I now do see that we can nothing know'.

That is the answer to a sum, it is the outcome of a long experience. But as Kierkegaard observed, it is quite a different thing when a freshman comes up to the university and uses the same sentiment to justify his indolence. As the answer to a sum it is perfectly true, but as the initial data it is a piece of self-deception. For acquired knowledge cannot be divorced from the existence in which it is acquired. The only man who has the right to say that he is justified by grace alone is the man who has left all to follow Christ. Such a man knows that the call to discipleship is a gift of grace, and that the call is inseparable from the grace. But those who try to use this grace as a dispensation from following Christ are simply deceiving themselves.

But, we may ask, did not Luther himself come perilously

near to this perversion in the understanding of grace? What about his *Pecca fortiter, sed fortius fide et gaude in Christo* ('Sin boldly, but believe and rejoice in Christ more boldly still')? You are a sinner, anyway, and there is nothing you can do about it. Whether you are a monk or a man of the world, a religious man or a bad one, you can never escape the toils of the world or from sin. So put a bold face on it, and all the more because you can rely on the *opus operatum* of grace. Is this the proclamation of cheap grace, naked and unashamed, the *carte blanche* for sin, the end of all discipleship? Is this a blasphemous encouragement to sin boldly and rely on grace? Is there a more diabolical abuse of grace than to sin and rely on the grace which God has given? Is not the Roman Cate-chism quite right in denouncing this as the sin against the Holy Ghost?

If we are to understand this saying of Luther's, everything depends on applying the distinction between the data and the answer to the sum. If we make Luther's formula a premiss for our doctrine of grace, we are conjuring up the spectre of cheap grace. But Luther's formula is meant to be taken, not as the premiss, but as the conclusion, the answer to the sum, the copingstone, his very last word on the subject. Taken as the premiss, *pecca fortiter* acquires the character of an ethical principle, a principle of grace to which the principle of *pecca fortiter* must correspond. That means the justification of sin, and it turns Luther's formula into its very opposite. For Luther 'sin boldly' could only be his very last refuge, the consolation for one whose attempts to follow Christ had taught him that he can never become sinless, who in his fear of sin despairs of the grace of God. As Luther saw it, 'sin boldly' did not happen to be a fundamental acknowledgement of his disobedient life; it was the gospel of the grace of God before which we are always and in every circumstance sinners. Yet that grace seeks us and justifies us, sinners though we are. Take courage and confess your sin, says Luther, do not try to run away from it, but believe more boldly still. You are a sinner, so be a sinner, and don't try to become what you are not. Yes, and become a sinner again and again every day, and be bold about it. But to whom can such words be addressed, except to those who from the bottom of their hearts make a daily renunciation of sin and of every barrier which hinders them from following Christ, but who nevertheless are troubled by their daily faithlessness and sin? Who can hear these words without endangering his faith but he who hears their consolation as a renewed summons to follow Christ? Interpreted in this way, these words of Luther become a testimony to the costliness of grace, the only genuine kind of grace there is.

Grace interpreted as a principle, *pecca fortiter* as a principle, grace at a low cost, is in the last resort simply a new law, which brings neither help nor freedom. Grace as a living word, *pecca fortiter* as our comfort in tribulation and as a summons to discipleship, costly grace is the only pure grace, which really forgives sins and gives freedom to the sinner.

We Lutherans have gathered like eagles round the carcase of cheap grace, and there we have drunk of the poison which has killed the life of following Christ. It is true, of course, that we have paid the doctrine of pure grace divine honours unparalleled in Christendom, in fact we have exalted that doctrine to the position of God himself. Everywhere Luther's formula has been repeated, but its truth perverted into self-deception. So long as our Church holds the correct doctrine of justification, there is no doubt whatever that she is a justified Church! So they said, thinking that we must vindicate our Lutheran heritage by making this grace available on the cheapest and easiest terms. To be 'Lutheran' must mean that we leave the following of Christ to legalists, Calvinists and enthusiasts—and all this for the sake of grace. We justified the world, and condemned as heretics those who tried to follow Christ. The result was that a nation became Christian and Lutheran, but at the cost of true discipleship. The price it was called upon to pay was all too cheap. Cheap grace had won the day.

But do we also realize that this cheap grace has turned back upon us like a boomerang? The price we are having to pay today in the shape of the collapse of the organized Church is only the inevitable consequence of our policy of making grace available to all at too low a cost. We gave away the word and sacraments wholesale, we baptized, confirmed, and absolved a whole nation unasked and without condition. Our humanitarian sentiment made us give that which was holy to the scornful and unbelieving. We poured forth unending streams of grace. But the call to follow Jesus in the narrow way was hardly ever heard. Where were those truths which impelled the early Church to institute the catechumenate which enabled a strict watch to be kept over the frontier between the Church and the world, and afforded adequate protection for costly grace? What had happened to those warnings of Luther's against preaching the gospel in such a manner as to make men rest secure in their ungodly living? Was there ever a more terrible or disastrous instance of the Christianizing of the world than this? What are those three thousand Saxons put to death by Charlemagne compared with the millions of spiritual corpses in our country today? With us it has been abundantly proved that the sins of the fathers are visited upon the children unto the third and fourth generations. Cheap grace has turned out to be utterly merciless to our Evangelical Church.

This cheap grace has been no less disastrous to our own spiritual lives. Instead of opening up the way to Christ it has closed it. Instead of calling us to follow Christ, it has hardened us in our disobedience. Perhaps we had once heard the gracious call to follow him, and had at this command even taken the first few steps along the path of discipleship in the discipline of obedience, only to find ourselves confronted by the word of cheap grace. Was that not merciless and hard? The only effect that such a word could have on us was to bar our way to progress, and seduce us to the mediocre level of the world, quenching the joy of discipleship by telling us that we were following a way of our own choosing, that we were spending our strength and disciplining ourselves in vain—all of which was not merely useless, but extremely dangerous. After all, we were told, our salvation had already been accomplished by the grace of God. The smoking flax was mercilessly extinguished. It was unkind to speak to men like this, for such a cheap offer could only leave them bewildered and tempt them from the way to which they had been called by Christ. Having laid hold on cheap grace, they were barred for ever from the knowledge of costly grace. Deceived and weakened, men felt that they were strong now that they were in possession of this cheap grace—whereas they had in fact lost the power to live the life of discipleship and obedience. The word of cheap grace has been the ruin of more Christians than any commandment of works.

In our subsequent chapters we shall try to find a message for those who are troubled by this problem, and for whom the word of grace has been emptied of all its meaning. This message must be spoken for the sake of truth, for those among us who confess that through cheap grace they have lost the following of Christ and further, with the following of Christ, have lost the understanding of costly grace. To put it quite simply, we must undertake this task because we are now ready to admit that we no longer stand in the path of true discipleship. We confess that, although our Church is orthodox as far as her doctrine of grace is concerned, we are no longer sure that we are members of a Church which follows its Lord. We must therefore attempt to recover a true understanding of the mutual relation between grace and discipleship. The issue can no longer be evaded. It is becoming clearer every day that the most urgent problem besetting our Church is this: How can we live the Christian life in the modern world?

Happy are they who have reached the end of the road we seek to tread, who are astonished to discover the by no means self-evident truth that grace is costly just because it is the grace of God in Jesus Christ. Happy are the simple followers of Jesus Christ who have been overcome by his grace, and are able to sing the praises of the all-sufficient grace of Christ with humbleness of heart. Happy are they who, knowing that grace, can live in the world without being of it, who, by following Jesus Christ, are so assured of their heavenly citizenship that they are truly free to live their lives in this world. Happy are they who know that discipleship simply means the life which springs from grace, and that grace simply means discipleship. Happy are they who have become Christians in this sense of the word. For them the word of grace has proved a fount of mercy.

(FROM: *The Cost of Discipleship*, pp. 35–47.)

3 POSITIVE CHRISTOLOGY

[A Christian doctrine of the Incarnation, Bonhoeffer insisted, must be realistic. This needs saying, he believed, because Christians have in their history hesitated to say, for instance, that Christ was born in the way that we are, or that he had exactly the same human nature as ours. On the latter point some Christians have said that the human nature assumed by Christ in the Incarnation was perfect ('unfallen'). Against this Bonhoeffer insists that Christians must make it quite clear that the Incarnation for them means that Christ shared in an unqualified way human nature as we know it. This meant among other things that there was an element of the incognito about the Incarnation. It was possible, that is, to mistake him for an ordinary man.]

1. *The Incarnate*

The question may not run 'How is it possible to conceive of the Incarnate?', but 'Who is he?' He is not adopted by God, and he is not clothed in human characteristics. He is the God who has become man as we have become man. He lacks nothing that is man's. There is nothing offered by this world or by men which Jesus Christ did not take. The protest against *enhypostasia*[1] must be maintained. Jesus Christ had his own human individual hypostasis[2] and human mode of existence. The man that I am, Jesus also was. Of him alone is it really true that nothing human remained alien to him. Of this man we say, 'This is God for us'.

This does not mean that we know, say, at an earlier stage quite apart from Jesus Christ, what and who God is, and then apply it to Christ. We have a direct statement of identity; whatever we can say here is prompted by a look at him, or, better, is compelled by this man. Neither does it mean that the statement 'This man is God' adds anything to his manhood. That is the essential point. *Per contra*, it could be argued that something was added to the man Jesus that we do not have, namely Godhead. And this is right. But we must be care-

[1] The idea that in the Incarnation Christ assumed human nature in general rather than the human nature of an individual. (Ed.)

[2] A difficult word to translate adequately: here almost 'personality'. (Ed.)

ful here. The union of God and man in Christ is not to be conceived of in terms of essence or *ousia*. The Godhead of Jesus is not an extension of his manhood. Nor it is something contiguous to his manhood, which Jesus goes on to achieve. The statement 'This man is God' touches on Jesus vertically from above. It takes nothing from him and adds nothing to him. It simply qualifies the whole man Jesus as God. It is God's judgement and Word on this man. But this qualification, this judgement and Word of God which 'comes from above' is in turn not to be thought of as something which is added. Rather than being understood as an addition, this Word of God coming from above is in fact the man Jesus Christ himself. And because Jesus Christ is also God's judgement on himself, he points at the same time both to himself and to God.

An attempt is thus made to avoid the union of two demonstrable isolated entities. Jesus, the man, is believed in as God. And he is believed in as the man, and not despite his manhood, or in addition to it. Faith in the Word ignites in the man Jesus. Jesus Christ is not God in a divine *ousia;* he is not God in a demonstable and describable way; he is God in faith. There is no such thing as this divine essence. If Jesus Christ is to be described as God, then we may not speak of this divine essence, of his omnipotence and his omniscience, but we must speak of this weak man among sinners, of his cradle and his cross. When we consider the Godhead of Jesus, then above all we must speak of his weakness. In christology one looks at the whole historical man Jesus and says of him, 'He is God'. One does not first look at a human nature and then beyond it to a divine nature; one meets the one man Jesus Christ, who is fully God.

The accounts of the birth and the baptism of Jesus stand side by side. The birth points wholly to Jesus himself. The baptism points to the Holy Spirit coming from above. The difficulty of taking the birth narrative and the baptism narrative together is a consequence of the doctrine of the two natures. But the two accounts are not a doctrine of two natures. If we disregard this doctrine, the one story deals with the presence of the Word of God in Christ and the other with the descent of the Word of God on Jesus. The child in the cradle is the whole God; see Luther's christology in the Christmas hymns. The call at the baptism is a confirmation of the first event; there is no adoptionism[1] in it. The cradle shows the man who is God, the baptism shows in respect of Jesus the God who calls.

So if we speak of Jesus Christ as God, we may not speak of him as the representative of an idea of God who possesses the properties of omniscience and omnipotence (there is no such thing as this abstract divine nature!); we must speak of his weakness, of the cradle and the cross; and this man is no abstract God.

Strictly speaking, we should really talk, not about the Incarnation, but only about the Incarnate One. An interest in the Incarnation raises the question 'How?' The question 'How?' thus underlies the hypothesis of the Virgin Birth. It is both historically and dogmatically questionable. The biblical evidence for it is uncertain. If the biblical evidence gave decisive evidence for the real fact, there might be no particular significance in the dogmatic obscurity. The doctrine of the Virgin Birth is meant to express the incarnation of God and not just the fact of the Incarnate One. But does it not miss the decisive point of the incarnation by implying that Jesus has *not* become man wholly as we are? The question remains open, just as and just because it is already open in the Bible.

The Incarnate One is the glorified God. 'The Word was made flesh and we beheld his glory.' God glorifies himself in man. That is the ultimate mystery of the Trinity. The humanity is taken up into the Trinity; not since eternity, but 'from now to all eternity'. The glorification of God in the flesh is now at the same time the glorification of man, who is to have life with the trinitarian God for eternity. So it is incorrect to see the incarnation of God as a judgement of God on man. God remains the Incarnate One even at the last judgement. The incarnation is the message of the glorification of God who sees his honour in being man. It must be observed that the incarnation is primarily a real revelation of the creator in the

[1] The idea that Jesus was an ordinary man who was 'adopted' into Godhead, rather like the divinization of heroes in Greek and Roman mythology. (Ed.)

creature, and not a veiled revelation. Jesus Christ is the unveiled image of God.

The incarnation of God may not be thought of as being derived from an idea of God where, say, the manhood already belongs to the idea of God as in the case of Hegel.[1] The biblical testimony, 'We saw his glory', is meant here. If the incarnation is thus regarded as the glorification of God we may go on again to slip in a speculative idea of God, which derives the incarnation as necessary from the idea of God. A speculative basis for the doctrine of the incarnation in an idea of God would pervert the free relationship between the creator and the creature into a logically necessary one. The incarnation is contingent. God freely binds himself to the creature, and freely glorifies himself in the Incarnate. Why does that sound strange and improbable? Because the revelation of the incarnation in Jesus Christ is not a visible glorification of God. Because this Incarnate one is also the Crucified.

2. *The Humiliated One and the Exalted One*

In considering humiliation and exaltation, we are not investigating the divine and human natures, but the way God exists as man. We do not know a Godhead and a manhood each in its own nature. We are concerned with the way in which the one who has been made man exists. Thus 'humiliation' does not mean a state where the Incarnate One is more man and less God, in other words a stage in the limitation of God. Neither does exaltation mean a state where he is more God and less man. In humiliation and exaltation, Jesus remains fully man and fully God. The statement 'This is God' must be made of the Humiliated One in just the same way as it is made of the Exalted One.

We say of the Humiliated One, 'This is God'. He makes none of his divine properties manifest in his death. On the contrary, all we see is a man doubting in God as he dies. But of this man we say, 'This is God'. Anyone who cannot do this does not know the meaning of 'God became man'. In the incarnation, God reveals himself without concealment. Not the Logos, the Godhead or the manhood of Christ, but the whole person of the God-man is in the humiliation. He veils himself

[1] G. W. F. Hegel (1770–1831), German philosopher. (Ed.)

in the concealment of this scandal. The principle of the humiliation is not Christ's humanity but the 'likeness of flesh' (Rom. 8:3). With the exaltation, this is done away with, but Christ's manhood remains eternal.

The question is no longer, *How* can God be humiliated man? but rather, *Who* is the humiliated God-man? The doctrine of the incarnation and the doctrine of the humiliation must be strictly distinguished from each other. The mode of existence of humiliation is an act of the Incarnate. That does not, of course, mean that he can be separated in time from the act of the incarnation; the God-man in history is always already the humiliated God-man, from the cradle to the cross.

In what way is this special mode of existence of the humiliation expressed? In the fact that Christ takes sinful flesh. The humiliation is made necessary by the world under the curse. The incarnation is relative to the first creation, the humiliation to fallen creation. In the humiliation, Christ enters the world of sin and death of his own free will. He enters it in such a way as to hide in it in weakness and not to be known as God-man. He does not enter in the royal clothes of a 'Form of God'. The claim which he raises as God-man in this form must provoke antagonism and hostility. He goes incognito as a beggar among beggars, as an outcast among the outcast, despairing among the despairing, dying among the dying. He also goes as sinner among the sinners, yet in that he is *peccator pessimus*[1] (Luther), as sinless among the sinners, And here the central problem of christology lies.

The doctrine of the sinlessness of Jesus is not one *locus* among others. It is a central point on which all that has been said is decided. The question runs: Did Jesus, as the humiliated God-man, fully enter into human sin? Was he a man with sins like ours? If not, was he then man at all? If not, can he then help at all? And if he was, how can he help us in our predicament, as he is in the same predicament?

It is vital here to understand what the 'likeness of flesh' can mean. It means the real image of human flesh. His flesh is our flesh. Liability to sin and self-will are an essential part of our flesh. Christ became involved in the predicament of the whole flesh. But to what extent does he differ from us? In the

---

[1] The worst sinner. (Ed.)

first place, not at all. He is man as we are, he is tempted on all sides as we are, indeed far more dangerously than we are. In his flesh, too, was the law that is contrary to God's will. He was not the perfectly good man. He was continually engaged in struggle. He did things which outwardly sometimes looked like like sin. He was angry, he was harsh to his mother, he evaded his enemies, he broke the law of his people, he stirred up revolt against the rulers and the religious men of his country. He entered man's sinful existence past recognition.

But everything depends on the fact that it is *he* who took the flesh with its liability to temptation and self-will. *He* did this and that, which seem to the onlooker to be sin and failure, and must be evaluated as such. Because it is *he*, these statements, of course, appear in a different light. It is really human flesh that he bore—but because *he* bears it, this flesh is robbed of its rights. He pronounces the verdict on his action. He has anguish as we do; it is his anguish. He is tempted as we are, but because *he* is condemned, we are saved through him. In the light of this 'He' the harshest and most scandalous expressions about this humiliated God-man must be ventured and tolerated. He was really made sin for us, and crucified as the *peccator pessimus*. Luther says that he is himself robber, murderer and adulterer as we are, for he bears our sin, and in so doing describes the ultimates foundation of all christological statements. As the one who bears our sin, and no one else, he is sinless, holy, eternal, the Lord, the Son of the Father.

There can be no balancing of the two expressions 'sinner' and 'sinless', as though one could still separate the Humiliated One from the likeness of flesh. He is fully man; he gives the law its due and is judged, *and* robs sin of its force. He is completely in the likeness of flesh and under condemnation as we are, and yet he is without sin. The likeness of flesh with its realm of sin is related to him, but it is related to him, who is yet without sin. Without reaching an equilibrium we must say: *He*, not the likeness of flesh, is without sin; but he does not will to be distinguished from this likeness of flesh. Christology cannot get round this paradox.

The assertion of the sinlessness of Jesus fails if it has in mind observable acts of Jesus. His deeds are done in the likeness of flesh. They are not sinless, but ambiguous. One can and should see good and bad in them. If a man wishes to be incognito, one insults him if one says to him: I have both seen you and seen through you (Kierkegaard). So we should not justify Jesus' sinlessness by his actions. The assertion of the sinlessness of Jesus in his actions is no demonstrable moral judgement but a statement of belief that it is *he* who does these ambiguous actions, *he* who is eternally without sin. Faith acknowledges that the One who is tempted, is the victor, the One who struggles is the Perfect One, the Unrighteous One is the Righteous One, the Rejected, the Holy One. Even the sinlessness of Jesus is incognito, 'Blessed is he who is not offended in me' (Matt. 11:6).

The humiliated God-man is a stumbling block for the Jews, i.e., or the pious man. His historical ambiguity is a stumbling block. The pious man, the righteous man does not act as *he* did. The claim which this man raises, that he is not only a pious man but the Son of God, is incomprehensible to the pious man because it breaks every law: 'The men of old have said ... but I ...' The authority he assumes is incomprehensible: 'But I say to you' (Matt. 5:21), and 'Your sins are forgiven you' (Matt. 9:2). That is the essence of the scandal. Were Jesus not wholly man, but of a divinized nature, the claim might well have been allowed. Had he done the signs which were demanded of him for proof, men would probably have believed in him. But just when it came to the point of signs and wonders, he retreated into his incognito and refused to give any visible attestation. In this way he makes a stumbling block. But everything depends on this. Had he answered the question put to him about his authority with a miracle, then it would not be true that he was wholly man as we are. At the decisive moment, in the question about Christ, the exception would have been made. So the nearer the revelation, the thicker the concealment must be; the more urgent the question about Christ, the more impenetrable the incognito.

That means that the form of scandal is the very one which makes belief in Christ possible. In other words, the form of humiliation is the form of the *Christus pro nobis*. In this Christ proved himself by miracles, we would 'believe' the visible theopathy of the Godhead, but it would not be belief in the *Christus pro me*. It would not be inner conversion, but acknowledgement. Belief in miracles is belief in a visible epiphany. Nothing happens in me if I assert my belief in miracles. There is only faith where a man so surrenders himself to the humiliated God-man as to stake his life on him, even when this seems against all sense. Faith is where the attempt to have security from something visible is rejected. In that case, it is faith in God and not in the world. The only assurance that faith tolerates is the Word itself which comes to me through Christ.

Anyone who looks for signs of verification remains by himself. He is not changed. Anyone who recognizes the Son through the scandal is a believer in the New Testament sense. He sees the *Christus pro nobis*, he is reconciled and made new. The stumbling block in the incognito and the ambivalent form of the *Christus pro nobis* is at the same time the unceasing temptation of faith. The temptation, however, teaches us to pay heed to the Word (Isa. 28:19). And from the Word comes faith.

How are we to understand the fact that Jesus nevertheless does miracles? Are they not a breaching of the incognito? If the incognito has once slipped, is it not all a mockery? Are we, with liberal theology, to regard miracle as a phenomenon of the age? Or must we not at least return to the doctrine of the two natures? Must we not recognize a *genus maiestaticum*?[1] The miracles are no breaching of the incognito. The ancient religious world is full of miracle workers and healers. Jesus is not alone in this. The realm of miracle is not identical with the realm of God. True, the miracles may exceed normal everyday happenings, but they are only on another level within the created world. The concept which goes with miracle is not that of God, but that of magic. Magic remains within the world. If Jesus does miracles, he preserves his incognito within the magical picture of the world. It is not miracle which accredits him as the Son of God in the New Testament. On the contrary, his authority is taken to be demonic.

Only the believing community recognizes the approach of the kingdom in the miracles of Jesus. It does not see only magic and false claims here. But the incognito is not done away

---

[1] *Genus maiestaticum*: a reference to the Lutheran teaching that in the Incarnate Christ the human nature took on divine attributes. (Ed.)

with for the unbeliever. The unbeliever sees magic and an ambiguous world. The believer says, 'Here is the kingdom of God.' Our age no longer lives in a magical world, but it is still inclined to take miracles as an unequivocal manifestation of the divine. But miracle remains ambiguous if it happens, and it needs to be explained. It *is* explained by both believer and unbeliever. The believer sees in it the prelude to the divine action at the end of the world. He sees, bound up with the incognito, something of the glory of God. 'We saw his glory' (John 1 : 14). But the non-believer sees nothing.

The Humiliated One is present to us only as the Risen and Exalted One. We know that he is the God-man in incognito only through the resurrection and the exaltation. As believers, we always have the incognito as an already penetrated incognito, we have the child in the cradle as the one who is eternally present, the one laden with guilt as the Sinless One. But the converse must also be valid. We cannot get round the scandal by means of the resurrection. We have the Exalted One only as the Crucified, the Sinless One only as the one laden with guilt, the Risen One only as the Humiliated One. Were this not so, the *pro nobis* would be done away with, there would be no faith. Even the resurrection is not a penetration of the incognito. Even the resurrection is ambiguous. It is only believed in where the stumbling block of Jesus has not been removed. Only the disciples who followed Jesus saw the resurrection. Only blind faith sees here. They believe as those who do not see, and in this faith they see. 'Blessed are they who do not see and yet believe' (John 20 : 29).

Between humiliation and exaltation the historical fact of the empty tomb lies oppressively starkly. What is the significance of the account of the empty tomb before the account of the resurrection? Is it the decisive fact of christology? If it was really empty, then is Christ not risen and our faith vain? It seems as though our faith in the resurrection were bound up with the account of the empty tomb. Is our faith then in the last resort only faith in the empty tomb?

This is and remains a last stumbling block which the person who believes in Christ must accept in one way or the other. Empty or not empty, it remains a stumbling block. We are not sure of its historicity. The Bible itself reveals the stumbling block in showing how hard it was to prove that the disciples had not perhaps stolen the body. Even here we cannot evade the realm of ambiguity. We cannot get round it anywhere. Jesus has entered even the testimony of Scripture in the form of a stumbling block. Even as the Risen One, he does not break through his incognito. He only breaks through it when he returns in glory. Then the Incarnate is no longer the Lowly One. Then the decision over faith and unbelief has already been made. Then the manhood of God is really and only the glorification of God.

We know all this now only from our encounter with the Lowly One. The Church goes its own way of lowliness with this Lowly One. It cannot strive for a visible confirmation of its way while it renounces itself at every step. But as the lowly Church, it may not look at itself in vain conceit, as though its its lowliness were visible proof that Christ was present there. Lowliness is no proof, at least it is not a proof that one can refer to. There is no law or principle here which the Church has to follow; this is a fact, in short, God's way with the Church. As Paul says of himself that he can be either exalted or lowly so long as it happens for the sake of Christ, so too the church can be exalted and lowly, so long as it follows Christ's way. This way is the enemy of the proud, whether they wrap themselves in purple robes or set the martyrs crown upon their heads. The Church always looks only to the humiliated Christ, whether it be exalted or lowly.

It is not good if the Church boasts of its lowliness too hastily. It is equally bad if it boasts of its power and influence too hastily.

It is only good if the Church humbly acknowledges its sins, allows itself to be forgiven and acknowledges its Lord. Every day it must receive the will of God afresh from Christ. It receives it because of the presence of the Incarnate, Lowly and Exalted One. Every day this Christ once again becomes a stumbling block for its own hopes and wishes. Every day it comes anew to the sentence, 'You will all be offended because of me' (Matt. 26:31), and every day it holds anew to the promise, 'Blessed is he who is not offended in me' (Matt. 11:6).

(FROM: *Christology*, pp. 106–18.)

3—MTS-5 * *

4 'ETHICS AS FORMATION'

[Bonhoeffer's *Ethics* is a significant attempt to reconstruct for the twentieth century the Christian ideal of the imitation of Christ. Every since Luther's criticism of it the *imitatio Christi* as an ethical pattern had been suspect in German protestantism. Luther criticized it because it had been taken in an antiquarian way as a literal attempt to mimic the Christ of the gospels. Luther also feared that it would be regarded as some kind of heroic moral endeavour to be like Christ which a man could attain by his own efforts apart from grace. For these reasons he preferred the term 'conformation to Christ' rather than 'imitation of Christ', as a way of bringing out that it is Christ, through the Spirit who brings Christians into some likeness to himself. Bonhoeffer takes up this phrase and seeks to show that far from being a vague abstract ideal it is embodied in the concrete realities of community and personal life and that conformation to Christ is compatible with the freedom and separate individuality of the human person.]

Conformation

The word 'formation' arouses our suspicion. We are sick and tired of Christian programmes and of the thoughtless and superficial slogan of what is called 'practical' Christianity as distinct from 'dogmatic' Christianity. We have seen that the formative forces in the world do not arise from Christianity at all and that the so-called practical Christianity is at least as unavailing in the world as is the dogmatic kind. The word 'formation', therefore, must be taken in quite a different sense from that to which we are accustomed. And in fact the Holy Scriptures speak of formation in a sense which is at first entirely unfamiliar to us. Their primary concern is not with the forming of a world by means of plans and pro-grammes. Whenever they speak of forming they are concerned only with the one form which has overcome the world, the form of Jesus Christ. Formation can come only from this form. But here again it is not a question of applying directly to the world the teaching of Christ or what are referred to as Christian principles, so that the world might be formed in accordance with these. On the contrary, formation come only by being drawn in into the form of Jesus Christ. It comes only as formation in His likeness, as *conformation* with the unique form of His who was made man, was crucified, and rose again.

This is not achieved by dint of efforts 'to become like Jesus', which is the way in which we usually interpret it. It is achieved only when the form of Jesus Christ itself works upon us in such a manner that it moulds our form in its own likeness (Gal. 4:19). Christ remains the only giver of forms. It is not Christian men who shape the world with their ideas, but it is Christ who shapes men in conformity with Himself. But just as we misunderstood the form of Christ if we take Him to be essentially the teacher of a pious and good life, so, too, we should misunderstand the formation of man if we were to regard it as instruction in the way in which a pious and good life is to be attained. Christ is the Incarnate, Crucified and Risen One whom the Christian faith confesses. To be transformed in His image (2 Cor. 3:18, Phil. 3:10, Rom. 8:29 and 12:2)—this is what is meant by the formation of which the Bible speaks.

To be conformed with the Incarnate—that is to be a real man. It is man's right and duty that he should be man. The quest for the superman, the endeavour to outgrow the man within the man, the pursuit of the herioc, the cult of the demigod, all this is not the proper concern of man, for it is untrue. The real man is not an object either for contempt or for deification, but an object of the love of God. The rich and manifold variety of God's creation suffers no violence here from false uniformity or from the forcing of men into the pattern of an ideal or a type or a definite picture of the human character. The real man is at liberty to be his Creator's creature. To be conformed with the Incarnate is to have the right to be the man one really is. Now there is no more pretence, no more hypcrisy or self-violence, no more compulsion to be something other, better and more ideal than what one is. God loves the real man. God became a real man.

To be formed in the likeness of the Crucified—this means being a man sentenced by God. In his daily existence man carries with him God's sentence of death, the necessity of dying before God for the sake of sin. With his life he testifies that nothing can stand before God save only under God's sentence and grace. Every day man dies the death of a sinner. Humbly he bears the scars on his body and soul, the marks of the wounds which sin inflicts on him. He cannot raise himself up above any other man or set himself to be the greatest of all sinners. He can excuse the sin of another, but never his own. He bears all the suffering imposed on him, in the knowledge that it serves to enable him to die with his own will and to accept God's judgement upon him. But in surrendering himself to God's judgement upon him and against him he is himself just in the eyes of God. In the words of K. F. Hartmann's poem, 'it is in suffering that the Master imprints upon our minds and hearts his own all-valid image'.

To be conformed with the Risen One—that is to be a new man before God. In the midst of death he is in life. In the midst of sin he is righteous. In the midst of the old he is new. His secret remains hidden from the world. He lives because Christ lives, and lives in Christ alone. 'Christ is my life' (Phil. 1:21). So long as the glory of Christ is hidden, so long, too, does the glory of his new life remain 'hidden with Christ in God' (Col. 3:3). But he who knows espies already here and there a gleam of what is to come. The new man lives in the world like any other man. Often there is little to distinguish him from the rest. Nor does he attach importance to distinguishing himself, but only to distinguishing Christ for the sake of his brethren. Transfigured though he is in the form of the Risen One, here he bears only the sign of the cross and the judgement. By bearing it willingly he shows himself to be the one who has received the Holy Spirit and who is united with Jesus Christ in incomparable love and fellowship.

The form of Jesus Christ takes form in man. Man does not take on an independent form of his own, but what gives him form and what maintains him in the new form is always solely the form of Jesus Christ Himself. It is therefore not a vain imitation or repetition of Christ's form but Christ's form itself which takes form in man, And again, man is not transformed into a form which is alien to him, the form of God, but into his own form, the form which is essentially proper to him. Man becomes man because God became man. But man does not become God. It is not he, therefore, who was or is able to accomplish his own transformation, but it is God who changes his form into the form of man, so that man may become, not indeed God, but, in the eyes of God, man.

In Christ there was re-created the form of man before God. It was an outcome of the place or the time, of the climate or the race, of the individual or the society, or of religion or of taste, but quite simply of the life of mankind as such, that mankind at this point recognized its image and its hope. What befell Christ had befallen mankind. It is a mystery, for which there is no explanation, that only a part of mankind recognize the form of their Redeemer. The longing of the Incarnate to take form in all men is as yet still unsatisfied. He bore the form of man as a whole, and yet He can take form only in a small band. These are His Church.

'Formation' consequently means in the first place Jesus's taking form in His Church. What takes form here is the form of Jesus Christ Himself. The New Testament states the case profoundly and clearly when it calls the Church the Body of Christ. The body is the form. So the Church is not a religious community of worshippers of Christ but is Christ Himself who has taken form among men. The Church can be called the Body of Christ because in Christ's Body man is really taken up by Him, and so too, therefore, are all mankind. The Church, then, bears the form which is in truth the proper form of all humanity. The image in which she is formed is the image of man. What takes place in her takes place as an example and substitute for all men. But it is impossible to state clearly enough that the Church, too, is not an independent form by herself, side by side with the form of Christ, and that she, too, can therefore never lay claim to an independent character, title, authority or dignity on her own account and apart from Him. The Church is nothing but a section of humanity in which Christ has really taken form. What we have here is utterly and completely the form of Jesus Christ and not some other form side by side with Him. The Church is the man in Christ, incarnate, sentenced and awakened to new life. In the first instance, therefore, she has essentially nothing whatever to do with the so-called religious functions of man, but with the whole man in his existence in the world with all its implications. What matters in the Church is not religion but the form of Christ, and its taking form amidst a band of men. If we allow ourselves to lose sight of this, even for an instant, we inevitably relapse into that programme-planning for the ethical or religious shaping of the world, which was where we set out from.

We have now seen that it is only with reference to the form that we can speak of formation in a Christian and ethical sense. Formation is not an independent process or condition which can in some way or other be detached from this form. The only formation is formation by and into the form of Jesus Christ. The point of departure for Christian ethics is the body of Christ, the form of Christ in the form of the Church, and formation of the Church in conformity with the form of Christ. The concept of formation acquires its significance, indirectly, for all mankind only if what takes place in the Church does in truth take place for all men. But this again does not mean that the Church is set up, so to speak, as a model for the world. One can speak of formation and of world only if mankind is called by name in its true form, which is its own by right, which it has already received, but which it merely fails to understand and accept, namely, the form of Jesus Christ, which is proper to man, and if in this way, in anticipation as one might say, mankind is drawn in into the Church. This means, then, that even when we speak in terms of the formation of the world we are referring solely to the form of Jesus Christ.

The form of Christ is one and the same at all times and in all places. And the Church of Christ also is one and the same throughout all generations. And yet Christ is not a principle in accordance with which the whole world must be shaped. Christ is not the proclaimer of a system of what would be good today, here and at all times. Christ teaches no abstract ethics such as must at all costs be put into practice. Christ was not essentially a teacher and legislator, but a man, a real man like ourselves. And it is not therefore His will that we should in our time be the adherents, exponents and advocates of a definite doctrine, but that we should be men, real men before God. Christ did not, like a moralist, love a theory of good, but He loved the real man. He was not, like a philosopher, interested in the 'universally valid', but rather in that which is of help to the real and concrete human being.

What worried Him was not, like Kant, whether 'the maxim of an action can become a principle of general legislation', but whether my action is at this moment helping my neighbour to become a man before God. For indeed it is not written that God became an idea, a principle, a programme, a universally valid proposition or a law, but that God became man. This means that though the form of Christ certainly is and remains one and the same, yet it is willing to take the form in the real man, that is to say, in quite different guises. Christ does not dispense with human reality for the sake of an idea which demands realization at the expense of the real. What Christ does is precisely to give effect to reality. He affirms reality. And indeed He is Himself the real man and consequently the foundation of all human reality. And so formation in conformity with Christ has this double implication. The form of Christ remains one and the same, not as a general idea but in its own unique character as the incarnate, crucified and risen God. And precisely for the sake of Christ's form the form of the real man is preserved, and in this way the real man receives the form of Christ.

The Concrete Place

This leads us away from any kind of abstract ethic and towards an ethic which is entirely concrete. What can and must be said is not what is good once and for all, but the way in which Christ takes form among us here and now. The attempt to define that which is good once and for all has, in the nature of the case, always ended in failure. Either the proposition was asserted in such general and formal terms that it retained no significance as regards its contents, or else one tried to include in it and elaborate the whole immense range of conceivable contents, and thus to say in advance what would be good in every single conceivable case; this led to a casuistic system so unmanageable that it could satisfy the demands neither of general validity nor of concreteness. The concretely Christian ethic is beyond formalism and casuistry. Formalism and casuistry set out from the conflict between the good and the real, but the Christian ethic can take for its point of departure the reconciliation, already accomplished, of the world with God and the man Jesus Christ and the acceptance of the real man by God.

But the question of how Christ takes form among us here and now, or how we are conformed with His form, contains within itself still further difficult questions. What do we mean by 'among us', 'now' and 'here'? If it is impossible to establish for all times and places what is good, then the question still arises for what times and places can any answer at all be given to our enquiry. It must not remain in doubt for a single moment that any one section to which we may now turn our attention is to be regarded precisely as a section, as a part of the whole of humanity. In every section of his history man is simply and entirely the man taken upon Himself by Christ. And for this reason whatever may have to be said about this section will always refer not only to this part but also to the whole. However, we must now answer the question regarding the times and places of which we are thinking when we set out to speak of formation through the form of Christ. These are in the first place quite generally the times and places which in some way concern us, those of which we have experience and which are reality for us. They are the times and places which confront us with concrete problems, set us tasks and charge us with responsibility. The 'among us', the 'now' and 'here' is therefore the region of our decisions and encounters. This region undoubtedly varies very greatly in extent according to the individual, and it might consequently be supposed that these definitions could in the end be interpreted so widely and vaguely as to make room for unrestrained individualism. What prevents this is the fact that by our history we are set objectively in a definite nexus of experiences, responsibilities and decisions from which we cannot free ourselves again except by an abstraction. We live, in fact, within this nexus, whether or not we are in every respect aware of it. Furthermore, this nexus is characterized in a quite peculiar manner by the fact that until our own days its consciously affirmed and recognized underlying basis has been the form of Christ. In our historical identity, therefore, we stand already in the midst of Christ's taking form, in a section of human history which He himself has chosen. It is consequently in this sense that we regard the west as the region for which we wish to speak and must speak, the world of the peoples of Europe and America in so far as it is already united through the form of Jesus Christ. To take a narrower view or to limit our consideration to Germany, for example, would be to lose sight of the fact that the form of Christ is the unity of the Western nations and that for this reason no single one of these nations can exist by itself or even be conceived as existing by itself. And to take a wider view would be to overlook the mysterious fact of the self-containedness of the Western world.

The purpose of what follows is not indeed to develop a programme for shaping or formation of the Western world. What is intended is rather a discussion of the way in which in this Western world the form of Christ takes form. This means that the discussion must be neither abstract nor casuistic, but entirely concrete. It must be insisted that no other form may be placed side by side with the form of Jesus Christ, for He alone is the subduer and reconciler of the world. Only this one form can help. And so whatever concrete assertion may have to be made here today about the way in which this form takes form amongst us, it must be referred quite strictly to this form of Jesus Christ. Moreover, in the incarnation of Christ the assurance is given us that Christ is willing to take form amongst us here and today.

Ethics as formation, then, means the bold endeavour to speak about the way in which the form of Jesus Christ takes form in our world, in a manner which is neither abstract nor casuistic, neither programmatic nor purely speculative. Concrete judgements and decisions will have to be ventured here. Decision and action can here no longer be delegated to the personal conscience of the individual. Here there are concrete commandments and instructions for which obedience is demanded.

Ethics as formation is possible only upon the foundation of the form of Jesus Christ which is present in His Church. The Church is the place where Jesus Christ's taking form is proclaimed and accomplished. It is this proclamation and this event that Christian ethics is designed to serve.

(FROM: *Ethics*, pp. 80–8.)

5 'THIS-WORLDLINESS AND OTHER-WORLDLINESS'

[Bonhoeffer believed that one of the urgent needs of the twentieth century was a reconstructed doctrine of the spiritual life. The word 'spiritual', however, he would have been suspicious of, because in Christian history it has often been assumed that that is most 'spiritual' which is most removed from the earthly, the material, the bodily, the sexual. This for Bonhoeffer constituted a radical denial of the Incarnation and, moreover, a blasphemous attempt to try and be more 'spiritual' than God who did not by-pass the material world but accepted it and used it.]

. . . And on the Christian aspect of the matter, there are some lines that say

> . . . that we remember what we would forget,
> that this poor earth is not our home.

That is indeed something essential, but it must come last of all. I believe that we ought so to love and trust God in our *lives*, and in all the good things that he sends us, that when the time comes (but not before!) we may go to him with love, trust, and joy. But, to put it plainly, for a man in his wife's arms to be hankering after the other world is, in mild terms, a piece of bad taste, and not God's will. We ought to find and love God in what he actually gives us; if it pleases him to allow us to enjoy some overwhelming earthly happiness, we mustn't try to be more pious than God himself and allow our happiness to be corrupted by presumption and arrogance, and by unbridled religious fantasy which is never satisfied with what God gives. God will see to it that the man who finds him in his earthly happiness and thanks him for it does not lack reminder that earthly things are transient, that it is good for him to attune his heart to what is eternal, and that sooner or later there will be times when he can say in all sincerity, 'I wish I were home'. But everything has its time, and the main thing is that we keep step with God, and do not keep pressing on a few steps ahead—nor keep dawdling a step behind. It's presumptuous to want to have everything at once—matrimonial bliss, the cross, and the heavenly Jerusalem, where they neither marry nor are given in marriage. 'For everything there is a season' (Eccles. 3 : 1); everything has its time: 'a time to weep, and a time to laugh; . . . a time to embrace, and a time to refrain from embracing; . . . a time to rend, and a time to sew; . . . and God seeks again what is past.' I suspect that these last words mean that nothing that is past is lost, that God gathers up again with us our past, which belongs to us. So when we are seized by a longing for the past—and this may happen when we least expect it—we may be sure that it is only one of the man 'hours' that God is always holding ready for us. So we oughtn't to seek the past again by our own efforts, but only with God . . .

. . . I think we honour God more if we gratefully accept the life that he gives us with all its blessings, loving it and drinking it to the full, and also grieving deeply and sincerely when we have impaired or wasted any of the good things of life (some people denounce such an attitude, and think it is bourgeois, weak, and sensitive), than if we are insensitive to life's blessings and may therefore also be insensitive to pain . . .

. . . What I mean is that God wants us to love him eternally with our whole hearts—not in such a way as to injure or weaken our earthly love, but to provide a kind of *cantus firmus*[1] to which the other melodies of life provide the counter-point. One of these contrapuntal themes (which have their own complete independence but are yet related to the *cantus firmus*) is earthly affection . . .

Now for some further thoughts about the Old Testament. Unlike the other oriental religions, the faith of the Old Testament isn't a religion of redemption. It's true that Christianity has always been regarded as a religion of redemption. But isn't this a cardinal error, which separates Christ from the Old Testament and interprets him on the lines of the myths about redemption? To the objection that a crucial importance is given in the Old Testament to redemption (from Egypt, and later from Babylon—cf. Deutero-Isaiah) it may be answered that the redemptions referred to here are *historical*, i.e., on *this* side of death, whereas everywhere else the myths about redemption are concerned to overcome the barrier of death.

[1] Basic theme. (Ed.)

Israel is delivered out of Egypt so that it may live before God as God's people on earth. The redemption myths try unhistorically to find an eternity after death. Sheol[1] and Hades are no metaphysical constructions, but images which imply that the 'past', while it still exists, has only a shadowy existence in the present.

The decisive factor is said to be that in Christianity the hope of resurrection is proclaimed, and that that means the emergence of a genuine religion of redemption, the main emphasis now being on the far side of the boundary drawn by death. But it seems to me that this is just where the mistake and the danger lie. Redemption now means redemption from cares, distress, fears, and longings, from sin and death, in a better world beyond the grave. But is this really the essential character of the proclamation of Christ in the gospels and by Paul? I should say it is not. The difference between the Christian hope of resurrection and the mythological hope is that the former sends a man back to his life on earth in a wholly new way which is even more sharply defined than it is in the Old Testament. The Christian, unlike the devotees of the redemption myths, has no last line of escape available from earthly tasks and difficulties into the eternal, but, like Christ himself ('My God, why hast thou forsaken me?'), he must drink the earthly cup to the dregs, and only in his doing so is the crucified and risen Lord with him, and he crucified and risen with Christ. This world must not be prematurely written off; in this the Old and New Testaments are at one. Redemption myths arise from human boundary-experiences, but Christ takes hold of a man at the centre of his life.

(FROM: *Letters and Papers from Prison*, pp. 168–9, 191–2, 303, 336–7.)

---

[1] Hebrew word for Hades. (Ed.)

6 'RELIGIONLESS CHRISTIANITY'

[In his later period Bonhoeffer pondered deeply on the question raised by Barth of the relationship between Christianity and religion (see Vol. 1, pp. 55 ff). Bonhoeffer suspected that religion is commonly thought of in a very primitive way as the satisfaction of the human need for security and significance and as a lazy way of dealing with the gaps in our knowledge. Hence the 'God of the gaps' type of religion where God is used as a term to fill in a gap in our ignorance which cannot yet be explained by scientific or other investigation. In all this, Bonhoeffer saw religion being used in relation to human weakness or ignorance, involving salvation *from* rather than *for* the world. He could see in Christianity however, the resources for a religion which relates to man in his strength, achievement and enterprise. He was moving towards a new version of man as made in the image of God: man as 'pro-creator' acting by and on behalf of the Creator to use and enjoy creation.]

. . . What is bothering me incessantly is the question what Christianity really is, or indeed who Christ really is, for us today. The time when people could be told everything by means of words, whether theological or pious, is over, and so is the time of inwardness and conscience—and that means the time of religion in general. We are moving towards a completely religionless time; people as they are now simply cannot be religious any more. Even those who honestly describe themselves as 'religious' do not in the least act up to it, and so they presumably mean something quite different by 'religious'.

Our whole nineteen-hundred-year-old Christian preaching and theology rest on the 'religious *a priori*' of mankind. 'Christianity' has always been a form—perhaps the true form—of 'religion'. But if one day it becomes clear that this *a priori* does not exist at all, but was a historically conditioned and transient form of human self-expression, and if therefore man becomes radically religionless—and I think that that is already more or less the case (else how is it, for example, that this war, in contrast to all previous ones, is not calling forth any 'religious' reaction?)—what does that mean for 'Christianity'?

It means that the foundation is taken away from the whole of what has up to now been our 'Christianity', and that there remain only a few 'last survivors of the age of chivalry', or a few intellectually dishonest people, on whom we can descend as 'religious'. Are they to be the chosen few? Is it on this dubious group of people that we are to pounce in fervour, pique, or indignation, in order to sell them our goods? Are we to fall upon a few unfortunate people in their hour of need and exercise a sort of religious compulsion on them? If we don't want to do all that, if our final judgement must be that the Western form of Christianity, too, was only a preliminary stage to a complete absence of religion, what kind of situation emerges for us, for the Church? How can Christ become the Lord of the religionless as well? Are there religionless Christians? If religion is only a garment of Christianity—and even this garment has looked very different at different times—then what is a religionless Christianity?

Barth, who is the only one to have started along this line of thought, did not carry it to completion, but arrived at a positivism of revelation,[1] which in the last analysis is essentially a restoration. For the religionless working man (or any other man) nothing decisive is gained here. The questions to be answered would surely be: What do a church, a community, a sermon, a liturgy, a Christian life mean in a religionless world? How do we speak of God—without religion, i.e., without the temporally conditioned presupposition of metaphysics, inwardness, and so on? How do we speak (or perhaps we cannot now even 'speak' as we used to) in a 'secular' way about 'God'? In what way are we 'religionless-secular' Christians, in what way are we the ἐκ-κλησία, those who are called forth, not regarding ourselves from a religious point of view as specially favoured, but rather as belonging wholly to the world? In that case Christ is no longer an object of religion, but something quite different, really the Lord of the world. But what does that mean? What is the place of worship and prayer in a religionless situation? Does the secret discipline, or alternatively the difference (which I have suggested to you before) between penultimate and ultimate, take on a new importance here? ...

[1] See Vol. 1, pp. 81 ff.

. . . The Pauline question whether περιτομή [circumcision] is a condition of justification seems to me in present-day terms to be whether religion is a condition of salvation. Freedom from περιτομή is also freedom from religion. I often ask myself why a 'Christian instinct' often draws me more to the religionless people than to the religious, by which I don't in the least mean with any evangelizing intention, but, I might almost say, 'in brotherhood'. While I'm often reluctant to mention God by name to religious people—because that name somehow seems to me here not to ring true, and I feel myself to be slightly dishonest (it's particularly bad when others start to talk in religious jargon; I then dry up almost completely and feel awkward and uncomfortable)—to people with no religion I can on occasion mention him by name quite calmly and as a matter of course. Religious people speak of God when human knowledge (perhaps simply because they are too lazy to think) has come to an end, or when human resources fail—in fact it is always the *deus ex machina* that they bring on to the scene, either for the apparent solution of insoluble problems, or as strength in human failure—always, that is to say, exploiting human weakness or human boundaries. Of necessity, that can go on only till people can by their own strength push these boundaries somewhat further out, so that God becomes superfluous as a *deus ex machina*. I've come to be doubtful of talking about any human boundaries (is even death, which people now hardly fear, and is sin, which they now hardly understand, still a genuine boundary today?). It always seems to me that we are trying anxiously in this way to reserve some space for God; I should like to speak of God not on the boundaries but at the centre, not in weaknesses but in strength; and therefore not in death and guilt but in man's life and goodness. As to the boundaries, it seems to me better to be silent and leave the insoluble unsolved. Belief in the resurrection is *not* the 'solution' of the problem of death. God's 'beyond' is not the beyond of our cognitive faculties. The transcendence of epistemological theory has nothing to do with the transcendence of God. God is beyond in the midst of our life. The Church stands, not at the boundaries where human powers give out, but in the middle of the village. That is how it is in the Old Testament, and in this sense we still read the

New Testament far too little in the light of the Old. How this religionless Christianity looks, what form it takes, is something that I'm thinking about a great deal.

A few more words about 'religionlessness'. I expect you remember Bultmann's essay on the 'demythologizing' of the New Testament?[1] My view of it today would be, not that he went 'too far', as most people thought, but that he didn't go far enough. It's not only the 'mythological' concepts, such as miracle, ascension, and so on (which are not in principle separable from the concepts of God, faith, etc.), but 'religious' concepts generally, which are problematic. You can't, as Bultmann supposes, separate God and miracle, but you must be able to interpret and proclaim *both* in a 'non-religious' sense. Bultmann's approach is fundamentally still a liberal one (i.e., abridging the gospel), whereas I'm trying to think theologically.

What does it mean to 'interpret in a religious sense'? I think it means to speak on the one hand metaphysically, and on the other hand individualistically. Neither of these is relevant to the biblical message or to the man of today. Hasn't the individualistic question about personal salvation almost completely left us all? Aren't we really under the impression that there are more important things than that question (perhaps not more important than the *matter* itself, but more important than the *question*!)? I know it sounds pretty monstrous to say that. But, fundamentally, isn't this in fact biblical? Does the question about saving one's soul appear in the Old Testament at all? Aren't righteousness and the Kingdom of God on earth the focus of everything, and isn't it true that Rom. 3:24 ff. is not an individualistic doctrine of salvation, but the culmination of the view that God alone is righteous? It is not with the beyond that we are concerned, but with this world as created and preserved, subjected to laws, reconciled, and restored. What is above this world is, in the gospel, intended to exist *for* this world; I mean that, not in the anthropocentric sense of liberal, mystic pietistic, ethical theology,

---

[1] 'New Testament and Mythology', Whitsun 1941, first printed in the supplements to *Evangelische Theologie* the same year; there is an English translation in *Kerygma and Myth* (ed. H. W. Bartsch), SPCK, p. 1–41. See Vol. 2, pp. 64 ff.

but in the biblical sense of the creation and of the incarnation, crucifixion, and resurrection of Jesus Christ.

Barth was the first theologian to begin the criticism of religion, and that remains his really great merit; but he put in its place a positivist doctrine of revelation which says, in effect, 'Like it or lump it': virgin birth, Trinity, or anything else; each is an equally significant and necessary part of the whole, which must simply be swallowed as a whole or not at all. That isn't biblical. There are degrees of knowledge and degrees of significance; that means that a secret discipline must be restored whereby the *mysteries* of the Christian faith are protected against profanation. The positivism of revelation makes it too easy for itself, by setting up, as it does in the last analysis, a law of faith, and so mutilates what is—by Christ's incarnation!—a gift for us. In the place of religion there now stands the Church—that is in itself biblical—but the world is in some degree made to depend on itself and left to its own devices, and that's the mistake.

. . . We are to find God in what we know, not in what we don't know; God wants us to realize his presence, not in unsolved problems but in those that are solved. That is true of the relationship between God and scientific knowledge, but it is also true of the wider human problems of death, suffering, and guilt. It is now possible to find, even for these questions, human answers that take no account whatever of God. In point of fact, people deal with these questions without God (it has always been so), and it is simply not true to say that only Christianity has the answers to them. As to the idea of 'solving' problems, it may be that the Christian answers are just as unconvincing—or convincing—as any others. Here again, God is no stop-gap; he must be recognized at the centre of life, not when we are at the end of our resources; it is his will to be recognized in life, and not only when death comes; in health and vigour, and not only in suffering; in our activities, and not only in sin. The ground for this lies in the revelation of God in Jesus Christ. He is the centre of life, and he certainly didn't 'come' to answer our unsolved problems.

(FROM: *Letters and Papers from Prison*, pp. 279–81, 281–2, 285–6, 311–12.)

7 'Man Come of Age'

[Bonhoeffer, in this extract, continues his reflections on the consequences for Christian belief of the realization that religion is not necessary for the underpinning of man's self-confidence. Christian apologists have often thought it essential to dwell on man's anxiety and despair before coming to the 'good news' of the gospel. In passing, Bonhoeffer calls in question Tillich's assumption that all men feel the pressure of certain 'ultimate questions' (life after death, judgement, etc.) which point towards religion. Increasingly, man 'come of age' is content to ignore such questions and because he has been brought up to expect God in the spectacular and astounding is ill-equipped to discover him in the ordinary and seemingly ineffectual.]

The movement that began about the thirteenth century (I'm not going to get involved in any argument about the exact date) towards the autonomy of man (in which I should include the discovery of the laws by which the world lives and deals with itself in science, social and political matters, art, ethics, and religion) has in our time reached an undoubted completion. Man has learnt to deal with himself in all questions of importance without recourse to the 'working hypothesis' called 'God'. In questions of science, art, and ethics this has become an understood thing at which one now hardly dares to tilt. But for the last hundred years or so it has also become increasingly true of religious questions; it is becoming evident that everything gets along without 'God'—and, in fact, just as well as before. As in the scientific field, so in human affairs generally, 'God' is being pushed more and more out of life, losing more and more ground.

Roman Catholic and Protestant historians agree that it is in this development that the great defection from God, from Christ, is to be seen; and the more they claim and play off God and Christ against it, the more the development considers itself to be anti-Christian. The world that has become conscious of itself and the laws that govern its own existence has grown self-confident in what seems to us to be an uncanny way. False developments and failures do not make the world doubt the necessity of the course that it is taking, or of its development; they are accepted with fortitude and detachment as part of the bargain, and even an event like the present war is no exception. Christian apologetic has taken the most varied forms of opposition to this self-assurance. Efforts are made to prove to a world thus come of age that it cannot live without the tutelage of 'God'. Even though there has been surrender on all secular problems, there still remain the so-called 'ultimate questions'—death, guilt—to which only 'God' can give an answer, and because of which we need God and the Church and the pastor. So we live, in some degree, on these so-called ultimate questions of humanity. But what if one day they no longer exist as such, if they too can be answered 'without God'? Of course, we now have the secularized offshoots of Christian theology, namely existentialist philosophy and the psychotherapists, who demonstrate to secure, contented, and happy mankind that it is really unhappy and desperate and simply unwilling to admit that it is in a predicament about which it knows nothing, and from which only they can rescue it. Wherever there is health, strength, security, simplicity, they scent luscious fruit to gnaw at or to lay their pernicious eggs in. They set themselves to drive people to inward despair, and then the game is in their hands. That is secularized methodism. And whom does it touch? A small number of intellectuals, of degenerates, of people who regard themselves as the most important thing in the world, and who therefore like to busy themselves with themselves. The ordinary man, who spends his everyday life at work and with his family, and of course with all kinds of diversions, is not affected. He has neither the time nor the inclination to concern himself with his existential despair, or to regard his perhaps modest share of happiness as a trial, a trouble, or a calamity.

The attack by Christian apologetic on the adulthood of the world I consider to be in the first place pointless, in the second place ignoble, and in the third place unchristian. Pointless, because it seems to me like an attempt to put a grown-up man back into adolescence, i.e., to make him dependent on things on which he is, in fact, no longer dependent, and thrusting him into problems that are, in fact, no longer problems to him. Ignoble, because it amounts to an attempt to exploit man's weakness for purposes that are alien to him and to which he has not freely assented. Unchristian, because it confuses Christ with one particular stage in man's religiousness, i.e., with a human law. More about this later.

But first, a little more about the historical position. The question is: Christ and the world that has come of age. The weakness of liberal theology was that it conceded to the world the right to determine Christ's place in the world; in the conflict between the Church and the world it accepted the comparatively easy terms of peace that the world dictated. Its strength was that it did not try to put the clock back, and that it genuinely accepted the battle (Troeltsch), even though this ended with its defeat.

Defeat was followed by surrender, and by an attempt to make a completely fresh start based on the fundamentals of the Bible and the Reformation. Heim[1] sought, along pietist and methodist lines, to convince the individual man that he was faced with the alternative 'despair or Jesus'. He gained 'hearts'. Althaus[2] (carrying forward the modern and positive line with a strong confessional emphasis) tried to wring from the world a place for Lutheran teaching (ministry) and Lutheran worship, and otherwise left the world to its own devices. Tillich set out to interpret the evolution of the world (against its will) in a religious sense—to give it its shape through religion. That was very brave of him, but the world unseated him and went on by itself; he, too, sought to understand the world better than it understood itself; but it felt that it was completely misunderstood, and rejected the imputation. (Of course, the world *must* be understood better than it understands itself, but not 'religiously' as the religious socialists wanted.)

Barth was the first to realize the mistake that all these attempts (which were all, in fact, still sailing, though unintentionally, in the channel of liberal theology) were making in leaving a clear space for religion in the world or against the world. He brought in against religion the God of Jesus Christ,

[1] Karl Heim, one of Bonhoeffer's theological teachers at Tübingen. (Ed.).
[2] Paul Althaus, German theologian who supported the Nazi-sponsored German Christians. (Ed.)

'*pneuma* against *sarx*'. That remains his greatest service (his *Epistle to the Romans*, second edition, in spite of all the neo-Kantian egg-shells). Through his later dogmatics, he enabled the Church to effect this distinction, in principle, all along the line. It was not in ethics, as is often said, that he subsequently failed—his ethical observations, as far as they exist, are just as important as his dogmatic ones—; it was that in the non-religious interpretation of theological concepts he gave no concrete guidance, either in dogmatics or in ethics. There lies his limitation, and because of it his theology of revelation has become positivist, a 'positivism of revelation', as I put it.

Now for a few more thoughts on our theme. I'm only gradually working my way to the non-religious interpretation of biblical concepts; the job is too big for me to finish just yet.

On the historical side: There is one great development that leads to the world's autonomy. In theology one sees it first in Lord Herbert of Cherbury,[1] who maintains that reason is sufficient for religious knowledge. In ethics it appears in Montaigne[2] and Bodin[3] with their substitution of rules of life for the commandments. In politics Machiavelli[4] detaches politics from morality in general and founds the doctrine of 'reasons of state'. Later, and very differently from Machiavelli, but tending like him towards the autonomy of human society, comes Grotius,[5] setting up his natural law as international law, which is valid *etsi deus non daretur*,[6] 'even if there were no God'. The philosophers provide the finishing touches: on the one hand we have the deism of Descartes,[7] who holds that the world is a mechanism, running by itself with no interference from God; and on the other hand the pantheism of Spinoza,[8] who says that God is nature. In the last resort, Kant[9] is a

[1] Lord Herbert of Cherbury (1583–1648), a forerunner of the English deists who held that reason and revelation were synonymous. (Ed.)

[2] Michel de Montaigne (1533–1592), French essayist. (Ed.)

[3] Jean Bodin (1530–1596), French political philosopher. (Ed.)

[4] Niccolo Machiavelli (1469–1527), Italian political philosopher. (Ed.)

[5] Hugo Grotius (1583–1645, Dutch jurist and theologian. (Ed.)

[6] 'without assuming there to be a God.' (Ed.)

[7] Réne Descartes (1596–1650), French philosopher and scientist. (Ed.)

[8] Baruch Spinoza (1632–77), Dutch Jewish philosopher. (Ed.)

[9] Immanuel Kant (1724–1804), German philosopher. (Ed.)

deist, and Fichte[1] and Hegel[2] are pantheists. Everywhere the thinking is directed towards the autonomy of man and the world.

(It seems that in the natural sciences the process begins with Nicolas of Cusa[3] and Giordano Bruno[4] and the 'heretical' doctrine of the infinity of the universe. The classical *cosmos* was finite, like the created world of the Middle Ages. An infinite universe, however it may be conceived, is self-subsisting, *etsi deus non daretur*. It is true that modern physics is not as sure as it was about the infinity of the universe, but it has not gone back to the earlier conceptions of its finitude.)

God as a working hypothesis in morals, politics, or science, has been surmounted and abolished; and the same thing has happened in philosophy and religion (Feuerbach!).[5] For the sake of intellectual honesty, that working hypothesis should be dropped, or as far as possible eliminated. A scientist or physician who sets out to edify is a hybrid.

Anxious souls will ask what room there is left for God now; and as they know of no answer to the question, they condemn the whole development that has brought them to such straits. I wrote to you before about the various emergency exits that have been contrived; and we ought to add to them the *salto mortale* [death-leap] back into the Middle Ages. But the principle of the Middle Ages is heteronomy in the form of clericalism; a return to that can be a counsel of despair, and it would be at the cost of intellectual honesty. It's a dream that reminds one of the song *O wüsst' ich doch den Weg zurück, den weiten Weg ins Kinderland.*[6] There is no such way—at any rate not if it means deliberately abandoning our mental integrity; the only way is that of Matt. 18:3,[7] i.e., through repentance, through *ultimate* honesty.

[1] Johann Gotlieb Fichte (1762–1814), German philosopher. (Ed.)

[2] G. W. F. Hegel (1770–1831), German philosopher. (Ed.)

[3] Nicolas of Cusa (*c.* 1400–64), German philosopher and mystic. (Ed.)

[4] Giordano Bruno (1548–1600), Italian philosopher. (Ed.)

[5] Ludwig Feuerbach (1804–72), German philosopher. (Ed.)

[6] 'If only I knew the way back, the long way into the land of childhood.'

[7] 'Unless you turn and become like children, you will never enter the kingdom of heaven.'

And we cannot be honest unless we recognize that we have to live in the world *etsi deus non daretur*. And this is just what we do recognize—before God! God himself compels us to recognize it. So our coming of age leads us to a true recognition of our situation before God. God would have us know that we must live as men who manage our lives without him. The God who is with us is the God who forsakes us (Mark 15:34).[1] The God who lets us live in the world without the working hypothesis of God is the God before whom we stand continually. Before God and with God we live without God. God lets himself be pushed out of the world on to the cross. He is weak and powerless in the world, and that is precisely the way, the only way, in which he is with us and helps us. Matt. 8:17[2] makes it quite clear that Christ helps us, not by virtue of his omnipotence, but by virtue of his weakness and suffering.

Here is the decisive difference between Christianity and all religions. Man's religiosity makes him look in his distress to the power of God in the world: God is the *deus ex machina*. The Bible directs man to God's powerlessness and suffering; only the suffering God can help. To that extent we may say that the development towards the world's coming of age outlined above, which has done away with a false conception of God, opens up a way of seeing the God of the Bible, who wins power and space in the world by his weakness. This will probably be the starting-point for our 'secular interpretation'.

(FROM: *Letters and Papers from Prison*, pp. 325–8, 359–61.)

---

[1] 'My God, my God, why hast thou forsaken me?'

[2] 'This was to fulfil what was spoken by the prophet Isaiah, "He took our infirmities and bore our diseases".'

8 'PARTICIPATION IN THE SUFFERING OF GOD'

[Christian theology in its classical phase would have shrunk from
all talk about 'the sufferings of God'. Suffering meant being acted
upon by exterior forces outside one's control and it was difficult
to see how one could reconcile belief in God's omnipotence and
self-sufficiency with talk about his 'suffering'. But there was the
problem of the crucifixion which necessitated Christians saying
that in some sense God suffered. Eastern orthodox theology has
always held that suffering in the sense of sacrificial self-giving
love is of the essence of God. God empties himself in creation,
in Incarnation and in re-creation (redemption). It seems that
Bonhoeffer was moving towards a fresh expression of this belief
in his presentation of the Christian life as one of self-giving love
in the real (not idealized or romanticized) world. This is to share in
the self-giving love of God who, at cost ('suffering') makes the
world genuinely real to himself by, for example, giving himself
to real history in Christ.]

. . . Man is summoned to share in God's sufferings at the
hands of a godless world.

He must therefore really live in the godless world, without
attempting to gloss over or explain its ungodliness in some
religious way or other. He must live a 'secular' life, and
thereby share in God's sufferings. He *may* live a 'secular' life
(as one who has been freed from false religious obligations
and inhibitions). To be a Christian does not mean to be
religious in a particular way, to make something of oneself (a
sinner, a penitent, or a saint) on the basis of some method or
other, but to be a man—not a type of man, but the man that
Christ creates in us. It is not the religious act that makes the
Christian, but participation in the sufferings of God in the
secular life. That is *metanoia*[1]: not in the first place thinking
about one's own needs, problems, sins, and fears, but allowing
oneself to be caught up into the way of Jesus Christ, into the
messianic event, thus fulfilling Isa. 53. Therefore 'believe in
the gospel', or, in the words of John the Baptist, 'Behold, the
Lamb of God, who takes away the sin of the world' (John

[1] 'Repentance'. (Ed.)

1:29). (By the way, Jeremias[1] has recently asserted that the Aramaic word for 'lamb' may also be translated 'servant'; very appropriate in view of Isa. 53!)

This being caught up into the messianic sufferings of God in Jesus Christ takes a variety of forms in the New Testament. It appears in the call to discipleship, in Jesus' table-fellowship with sinners, in 'conversions' in the narrower sense of the word (e.g., Zacchaeus), in the act of the woman who was a sinner (Luke 7)—an act that she performed without any confession of sin, in the healing of the sick (Matt. 8:17; see above), in Jesus' acceptance of children. The shepherds, like the wise men from the East, stand at the crib, not as 'converted sinners', but simply because they are drawn to the crib by the star just as they are. The centurion of Capernaum (who makes no confession of sin) is held up as a model of faith (cf. Jairus). Jesus 'loved' the rich young man. The eunuch (Acts 8) and Cornelius (Acts 10) are not standing at the edge of an abyss. Nathaniel is 'an Israelite indeed, in whom there is no guile' (John 1:47). Finally, Joseph of Arimathea and the women at the tomb. The only thing that is common to all these is their sharing in the suffering of God in Christ. That is their 'faith'. There is nothing of religious method here. The 'religious act' is always something partial; 'faith' is something whole, involving the whole of one's life. Jesus calls men, not to a new religion, but to life.

But what does this life look like, this participation in the powerlessness of God in the world? I will write about that next time, I hope. Just one more point for today. When we speak of God in a 'non-religious' way, we must speak of him in such a way that the godlessness of the world is not in some way concealed, but rather revealed, and thus exposed to an unexpected light. The world that has come of age is more godless, and perhaps for that very reason nearer to God, than the world before its coming of age.

I discovered later, and I'm still discovering right up to this moment, that it is only by living completely in this world that one learns to have faith. One must completely abandon any attempt to make something of oneself, whether it be a saint,

[1] Joachim Jeromias, contemporary German New Testament Scholar. (Ed.)

or a converted sinner, or a churchman (a so-called priestly type!), a righteous man or an unrighteous one, a sick man or a healthy one. By this-worldliness I mean living unreservedly in life's duties, problems, successes and failures, experiences and perplexities. In so doing we throw ourselves completely into the arms of God, taking seriously, not our own sufferings, but those of God in the world—watching with Christ in Gethsemane. That, I think, is faith; that is *metanoia*; and that is how one becomes a man and a Christian (cf. Jer. 45!). How can success make us arrogant, or failure lead us astray, when we share in God's sufferings through a life of this kind?

(FROM : *Letters and Papers from Prison*, pp. 361–2, 369–70.)

9 'OUTLINE FOR A BOOK'

[This extract gives the famous synopsis of a book which Bonhoeffer was planning to write. This was obviously going to expand his thoughts on 'man's coming of age', 'wordliness', Christ as 'the man for others', and the church as the 'servant' imitator of Christ. Already there have been many attempts to finish Bonhoeffer's book for him but one has the feeling that like Schubert's 'Unfinished Symphony' the 'Outline for a book' will remain one of the great fragments of human endeavour.]

I should like to write a book of not more than 100 pages, divided into three chapters:

1. A Stocktaking of Christianity.
2. The Real Meaning of Christian Faith.
3. Conclusions.

Chapter 1 to deal with:

(*a*) The coming of age of mankind (as already indicated). The safeguarding of life against 'accidents' and 'blows of fate'; even if these cannot be eliminated, the danger can be reduced. Insurance (which, although it lives on 'accidents', seeks to mitigate their effects) as a western phenomenon. The aim: to be independent of nature. Nature was formerly conquered by spiritual means, with us by technical organization of all kinds. Our immediate environment is not nature, as formerly, but organization. But with this protection from nature's menace there arises a new one—through organization itself.

But the spiritual force is lacking. The question is: What protects us against the menace of organization? Man is again thrown back on himself. He has managed to deal with everything, only not with himself. He can insure against everything, only not against man. In the last resort it all turns on man.

(*b*) The religionlessness of man who has come of age. 'God' as a working hypothesis, as a stop-gap for our embarrassments, has become superfluous (as already indicated).

(*c*) The Protestant church: Pietism as a last attempt to maintain evangelical Christianity as a religion; Lutheran orthodoxy, the attempt to rescue the Church as an institution for salvation; the Confessing Church: the theology of revelation; a δὸς μοὶ ποῦ στῶ[1] over against the world, involving a 'factual' interest in Christianity; art and science searching for their origin. Generally in the Confessing Church: standing up for the Church's 'cause', but little personal faith in Christ. 'Jesus' is disappearing from sight. Sociologically: no effect on the masses—interest confined to the upper and lower middle classes. A heavy incubus of difficult traditional ideas. The decisive factor; the Church on the defensive. No taking risks for others.

(*d*) Public morals—as shown by sexual behaviour.

Chapter 2.

(*a*) God and the secular.

(*b*) Who is God? Not in the first place an abstract belief in God in his omnipotence etc. That is not a genuine experience of God but a partial extension of the world. Encounter with Jesus Christ. The experience that a transformation of all human life is given in the fact that 'Jesus is there only for others'. His 'being there for others' is the experience of transcendence. It is only this 'being there for others', maintained till death, that is the ground of his omnipotence, omniscience,

[1] 'Grant me to be able to stand.' (Ed.)

and omnipresence. Faith is participation in this being of Jesus (incarnation, cross, and resurrection). Our relation to God is not a 'religious' relationship to the highest, most powerful, and best Being imaginable—that is not authentic transcendence—but our relation to God is a new life in 'existence for others', through participation in the being of Jesus. The transcendental is not infinite and unattainable tasks, but the neighbour who is within reach in any given situation. God in human form—not, as in oriental-religions, in animal form, monstrous, chaotic, remote, and terrifying, nor in the conceptual forms of the absolute, metaphysical, infinite, etc., nor yet in the Greek divine human form of 'man in himself', but 'the man for others', and therefore the Crucified, the man who lives out of the transcendent.

(*c*) Interpretation of biblical concepts on this basis. (Creation, fall, atonement, repentance, faith, the new life, the last things.)

(*d*) Cultus. (Details to follow later, in particular on cultus and 'religion'.)

(*e*) What do we really believe? I mean, believe in such a way that we stake our lives on it? The problem of the Apostles' Creed? 'What *must* I believe?' is the wrong question; antiquated controversies, especially those between the different sects; the Lutheran versus Reformed,[1] and to some extent the Roman Catholic versus Protestant, are now unreal. They may at any time be revived with passion, but they no longer carry conviction. There is no proof of this, and we must simply take it that it is so. All that we can prove is that the faith of the Bible and Christianity does not stand or fall by these issues. Karl Barth and the Confessing Church have encouraged us to entrench ourselves persistently behind the 'faith of the Church', and evade the honest question as to what we ourselves really believe. That is why the air is not quite fresh, even in the Confessing Church. To say that it is the Church's business, not mine, may be a clerical evasion, and outsiders always regard it as such. It is much the same with the dialectical assertion that I do not control my own faith, and that it is therefore not for me to say what my faith is. There may be a place for all these considerations, but they do

[1] i.e., Calvinist. (Ed.)

not absolve us from the duty of being honest with ourselves. We cannot, like the Roman Catholics, simply identify ourselves with the Church. (This, incidentally, explains the popular opinion about Roman Catholics' insincerity.) Well then, what do we really believe? Answer: see (*b*), (*c*), and (*d*).

Chapter 3.

Conclusions:

The Church is the Church only when it exists for others. To make a start, it should give away all its property to those in need. The clergy must live solely on the free-will offerings of their congregations, or possibly engage in some secular calling. The Church must share in the secular problems of ordinary human life, not dominating, but helping and serving. It must tell men of every calling what it means to live in Christ, to exist for others. In particular, our own Church will have to take the field against the vices of *hubris*, power-worship, envy, and humbug, as the roots of all evil. It will have to speak of moderation, purity, trust, loyalty, constancy, patience, discipline, humility, contentment, and modesty. It must not underestimate the importance of human example (which has its origin in the humanity of Jesus and is so important in Paul's teaching); it is not abstract argument, but example, that gives its word emphasis and power. (I hope to take up later this subject of 'example' and its place in the New Testament; it is something that we have almost entirely forgotten.) Further: the question of revising the creeds (the Apostles' Creed); revision of Christian apologetics; reform of the training for the ministry and the pattern of clerical life.

All this is very crude and condensed, but there are certain things that I'm anxious to say simply and clearly—things that we so often like to shirk. Whether I shall succeed is another matter, especially if I cannot discuss it with you. I hope it may be of some help for the Church's future.

(FROM: *Letters and Papers from Prison*, pp. 380–3).

FOR FURTHER STUDY AND DISCUSSION

1 Throughout his theology, Bonhoeffer was concerned with the nature and rôle of the Church. On the one hand he had a high doctrine of the Church as 'the formation of Christ', and on the other an acute sense of how certain images of the Church (as the 'great lord', for example, or the holder of all certain truth) could get in the way. Is Bonhoeffer's image of the Church as the 'servant' adequate? Can one relate the concept of the 'Body of Christ' to the empirical Church?

2 Bonhoeffer's *Ethics* attempts to relate belief about Christ to Christian ethics and the pattern of the Christian life. Is this the way to bring out the distinctive character of the Christian conception of the good life?

3 Is it sufficient to think of Christ as 'the man for others'? How does this relate to traditional Christian teaching about Christ?

4 Imagine you had invited Barth, Tillich, Bultmann and Bonhoeffer for an evening and the conversation turned to the subject of the meaning of the Bible for modern man. How do you think the conversation would have gone?

5 Did Bonhoeffer in his interpretation of the Christian life as 'a participation in the sufferings of God' run the risk of turning Christianity into a tragedy?

6 Can Christianity do without 'religion'?

FOR FURTHER READING

THE LIFE OF BONHOEFFER

1965 *No Rusty Swords* (Collected Works. Volume I).
1966 *The Way to Freedom* (Collected Works. Volume II).
1966 *I Knew Dietrich Bonhoeffer* (edited by W. D. Zimmermann and R. G. Smith).
1968 Mary Bosanquet, *The Life and Death of Dietrich Bonhoeffer*.
1970 E. Bethge, *Dietrich Bonhoeffer* (likely to remain the standard biography).

PRINCIPAL WORKS OF BONHOEFFER

Sanctorum Communio (Berlin and Frankfurt/Oder 1930 ET 1963).
Act and Being (Munich 1956) ET 1962.
Christology (Munich 1960) ET 1960.
Creation and Temptation (Munich 1937 and 1953) ET 1955 and 1959.
The Cost of Discipleship (Munich 1937) ET 1948.
Life Together (Munich 1939) ET 1954.
Ethics (Munich 1949) ET 1955.
Letters and Papers from Prison (Munich 1951) ET 1955.

SOME BOOKS ABOUT BONHOEFFER

A. Dumas, *Dietrich Bonhoeffer : theologian of reality*, 1971. (To date the best book on Bonhoeffer's theology.)
Martin E. Marty (ed.), *The Place of Bonhoeffer*, 1963.
R. Gregor Smith (ed.), *World Come of Age*, 1967. (Contains the valuable Chicago lectures of Eberhard Bethge on 'The Challenge of Dietrich Bonhoeffer's Life and Theology' and important comments on Bonhoeffer by Barth and Bultmann.)
John A. Phillips, *The Form of Christ in the World*, 1967. (A study of Bonhoeffer's Christology.)

FOR GENERAL BACKGROUND READING

John Macquarrie, *Twentieth-century Religious Thought*, 1963.
——, *God-talk*, 1967.
——, *God and Secularity*, 1968.
Frederick Ferré, *Language, Logic and God*, 1962.
——, *Basic Modern Philosophy of Religion*, 1968.
David E. Jenkins, *Guide to the Debate about God*, 1966.
Colin Williams, *Faith in a Secular Age*, 1966.
E. L. Mascall, *The Secularisation of Christianity*, 1965.
H. Gollwitzer, *The Existence of God as confessed by faith*,
A. M. Ramsey, *God, Christ and the World*, 1969.
    1964.
T. W. Ogletree, *The Death of God Controversy*, 1966.